# Aroha

Māori wisdom for a contented life
lived in harmony with our planet

EBURY
PRESS

DR HINEMOA ELDER

E te kāhu kōrako, ko koe te whare o te whakaaro nui.
Inspired by Te Wharehuia Milroy, our wise and learned teacher.

Tika tāu kōrero, 'Āe, kaua rānei. Kāore he me whakamātau'.
As you quite rightly said, 'Yes or no, there is no such thing as try, just do'.

E ngā kuku o te manawa, Millie Tanerore kōrua ko Reuben Apirana, e ngā rangatira katoa mō āpōpō, e taku koroua, Huatahi, e ngā tamariki mokopuna, e ngā mātua tūpuna, e ngā mātua kēkē, e ngā whanaunga, e ngā hoa, e ngā kiritata o te hapori, e ngā pou whakawhirinaki mai rā anō, kia kai koutou i tēnei momo kai tuku iho hei oranga mō tātou, hei oranga anō mō Papatūānuku rāua ko Tangaroa.

*A note on design*: The illustrations for *Aroha* were created by New Zealand artists Harmony Repia (Ngāti Porou) and Luther Ashford (Ngāti Ruanui, Ngā Rauru), each inspired by the traditional decoration, *kōwhaiwhai*, often found in *whare nui*, Māori meeting houses. The cover includes a photograph of protective and precious Māori *pounamu*, known as greenstone, only found on Te Wai Pounamu, South Island, Aotearoa, New Zealand. Each chapter opener is different to denote the chapter's themes and is inspired by *toi whakairo*, the Māori art of carving, and *tā moko*, on the skin.

# Contents

Aroha – An introduction  1

*Manaakitanga
– te aroha ki te tangata*  13
Care, respect and kindness towards others and ourselves

*Kaitiakitanga
– te aroha ki a Papatūānuku*  67
Love for our world

*Whanaungatanga
– te aroha ki ngā hononga*  117
Empathy and connection between people

*Tino rangatiratanga
– te aroha ki te tika*  171
The pursuit of what is right, self-determination

*Kupu whakatepe / Conclusion*  223
*Index*  225
*He Puna whakataukī/whakatauākī*  229
*He mihi / Acknowledgements*  231
*About the Author*  233

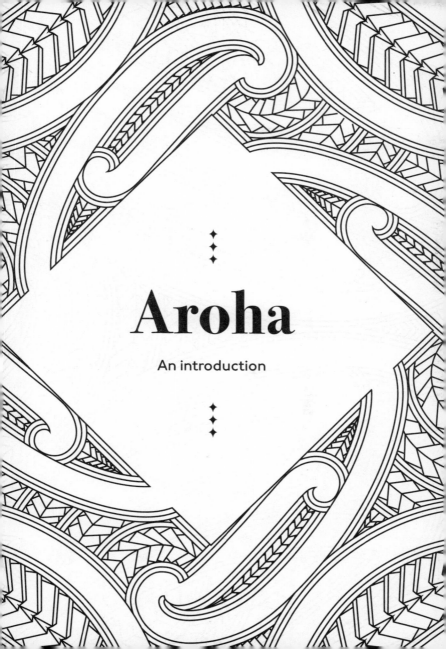

# Aroha

An introduction

# An Introduction

*Ko Pārengarenga te moana.*
Pārengarenga is my ocean.

*Ko Tawhitirahi te maunga.*
Tawhitirahi is my mountain.

*Ko Awapoka te awa.*
Awapoka is my river.

*Ko Kurahaupō te waka.*
Kurahaupō is my ancestral canoe.

*Ko Pōtahi rāua ko Te Reo Mihi ōku marae.*
Pōtahi and Te Reo Mihi are my traditional
meeting places.

*Ko Te Aupōuri, ko Ngāti Kurī, ko Te Rarawa,
ko Ngāpuhi nui tonu ōku iwi.*
My tribes are Te Aupōuri, Ngāti Kurī, Te Rarawa
and Ngāpuhi.

*Ko Hinemoa taku ingoa.*
My name is Hinemoa.

**Kia ora,** welcome to your book of *Aroha*, Māori proverbial sayings to open your heart, for a more thoughtful and resourceful you and a better world.

I am a child and adolescent psychiatrist from Aotearoa, the land of the long white cloud. You might know our lands as New Zealand.

This book is filled with *aroha* embedded in *whakataukī*, Māori proverbs, some of them very old, passed on by our ancestors because they give insight and life lessons still very relevant in our complex modern world.

*Aroha* is an ancient Māori word and concept. The word describes a deeply felt emotion and a way of thinking that encompasses love, compassion, sympathy and empathy. We consider *aroha* as something that comes from somewhere deep within us, and all around us, an inexhaustible source, a divine wellspring you might say.

I have been wanting to share this source of *aroha* for a long time because I see a loss of connection to it. In my daily work as a psychiatrist I see so many people deeply affected by the complex stress and trauma of life. I see my friends and *whānau* (extended family) struggling to make sense of the realities of our earth's warming and the devastating impact of human destruction on the planet. I notice how much healing and joy we gain from looking after our local environment, alongside it benefiting the world.

A few years ago I started writing a weekly newspaper column. I included a *whakataukī* every week, to keep my writing true to the wisdom of our ancestors. It was then that I realised *whakataukī* are a portal, a doorway into the ancient, sacred energy of *aroha*, the timeless wisdom of Māori culture.

So what are these *whakataukī*?

They are nuggets of wisdom that provide life lessons, guidance, notes of caution, sometimes a source of comfort. They stem from the great story-telling traditions of Māori culture. They remind us of the potency of Māori values and how and why to put them into action.

We Māori believe that we are intimately bound to our land. Our word for placenta is the same as our word for land, *whenua*. This dual use signals our profound connection with both types of *whenua*. The placenta is commonly buried in homelands as a physical manifestation of a person's intimate connection to the lands of our ancestors. We call ourselves *tangata whenua*, people of the land. We identify ourselves by the history of our lands, oceans, rivers and lakes. Without our lands we do not exist – in our world view, we are the land and the land is us.

Our language, *te reo Māori*, is at the heart of how we express our unique ways of thinking and feeling, our ways of being. We value rituals of meeting and hospitality, which are encompassed by the word *manaaki*. We need to know the blood ties and other links of connection to the people around us, something we call *whanaungatanga*. These are the aspects of our world that uphold our sense of wellbeing, our connection with all aspects of the universe. We call our sense of wellbeing our *wairua* – this is our spirit, our soul.

This book brings Māori *whakataukī* (pronounced far-car-tow-key, emphasis on 'key'), indigenous New Zealand proverbial sayings, into homes around the world. One for every week of the year.

I have chosen each of these pithy, wise *whakataukī* with great care. They are steeped in the ancient, undiluted concentrate of learnings necessary for survival. They mean so much to me. Many have helped me through challenging periods in my life. Some have been a means to hold on through a particularly tough day. The modern translations are my own interpretation of how these *whakataukī* have come to life for me. Other meanings may emerge for you. This is the power of *whakataukī*. They open up new thinking, they open up the heart, and a myriad of possibilities, manifestations of *aroha* that are deeply personal.

Why do we need *whakataukī*?

Our own health, and our mental health in particular, is intimately connected to our experiences of the world. This is evident from studies looking at the impact of emotional reciprocity in our earliest days, studies of trauma and of the health benefits of being in nature. As we witness change beyond our control, and experience uncertainty, stress, anxiety and fear for our futures, we are also on a continuous quest for calm, happiness and peace. When we face so much to be fearful of, how and where can we find solace, renewed vigour, or a sense of hope?

At the same time, finding and fostering lasting love in our lives, nurturing healthy family relationships, feeling a sense of security and living a healthy and contented life – the simple things – can seem so complicated to achieve.

The way we communicate our values and build relationships with each other is changing at an ever-accelerating pace. It is hard to keep up. Most of us have an online life in some capacity or other alongside our real lives. In this online life we have to contend with issues like 'fake news' and 'trolling', artificial intelligence, virtual and augmented realities, 'friends' we have never met in person. And body images that can make us feel insecure. All in the palm of your hand, intruding into your home, into your day, without a key, like uninvited guests. It is not surprising that, at times, it seems an impossible task to find a sense of peace.

And our relationship with the world is in flux. Evidence is irrefutably showing that we are living with real consequences of the damage we have caused to our lands and waters. Our climate is rapidly changing, our lands are being washed away, some are being submerged, and our life-giving waters are being contaminated or are disappearing by our own hand. We face border closures, pandemics – how we adapt to the ripple effects on our communities can catch us off guard. What it means for each of us to stay safe and take care of ourselves and our families has changed.

This book provides an alternative perspective with which to view our world, our place within it, and how we live alongside one another. It is a perspective that stems from ancient times and remains acutely relevant for today's world.

My experience working with patients, their families and with communities as a Māori psychiatrist is that when we are better connected to the world around us, with the community we live in, and are supported by and supportive of our neighbours, we are better protected from distress and fear. This is the long-held Māori belief and way of living. And when we remind ourselves who we are, through these touchstones, we are protected from mental distress and we can find strength to heal a multitude of mental and emotional wounds.

On a physical level, simple things like being close to nature have been proven to slow our breathing and lower our blood pressure. At the same time, we are more likely to stop, notice and value our surroundings, allowing our busy minds to pause.

We might then feel the impulse to protect the nature around us when we stop and notice evidence of disruption of harmony in the natural world, and feel the very real flow-on benefits of these activities for ourselves and those we are close to. We are more likely to pick up rubbish, more likely to pay attention to activities that harm our environment and work to stop these – championing the reduction of single-use plastics, lobbying for reduced emissions, replanting river banks, considering our own purchases and what impact they might have on the world.

Our Māori ancestors held fast to their own values and beliefs. This is how they survived and thrived after traversing the largest ocean in the world and settling in the furthest corner of Te Moana-nui-a-Kiwa, the Pacific Ocean, in the small place we call Aotearoa, New Zealand, more than a thousand years ago. These ways of thinking and living have been passed on through *whakataukī*. These treasures have remained, this form of transmitting our values has persisted because *whakataukī* continue to have compelling relevance today. It is exciting to witness from time to time that new *whakataukī* are written in the ancient tradition, keeping this practice alive.

Dip into the book. Choose a *whakataukī* for your week. Whether you are on the train, cuddled up in bed or waiting to pick up the kids from school. Take a moment each day to think about what this *whakataukī* could mean for you, in your current situation, with regard to the questions you have about yourself and your life.

Take a breath. Take in the *aroha*. Trust the *whakataukī* to help you find new possibilities, new ways of thinking, to heal in life. These sayings have hidden insights that will reveal different things at different times. So have fun with the book and stay open to the changing discoveries and insights of these sayings rich with ancient wisdom.

(A *whakataukī* is a proverbial saying where the originator is unknown. A *whakatauākī* is a proverbial saying with a known originator.)

# Manaakitanga

**Te aroha ki te tangata**

**Manaaki** is one of the cornerstones of our Māori world view. It expresses the very essence of respectful caring and protection of others. *Manaaki* upholds generosity and providing hospitality. It is seen in the way that we take *kai*, food, to others' homes when we visit, in the way we take off our shoes at our homes and in many formal cultural meetings. It can be experienced on the *marae*, traditional meeting places. *Manaaki* is perhaps most evident with the provision of shared food after the formalities are completed, the importance of everyone having plenty to eat and the food being delicious. *Manaaki* is about the subtle and intuitive kindness in the touch of the hand, the hug, recognising each other's losses, pain and triumphs. *Manaaki* is about the *aroha* of eye contact. We need to take care of ourselves in order to provide *manaaki*; in order to be tuned in to others' needs, we must also be in a state of wellbeing in relation to ourselves.

# 1

# Tūwhitia te hopo!

## Banish your fears!

**Feel the fear and do it anyway!**

A well-known modern English phrase whose sentiment has existed for many years in this *whakataukī*.

I feared being exposed as an imposter. I was afraid of being found unworthy. I was fearful of not being enough. I had a deep fear of being less than capable. But I have discovered something very simple. These are the very things that, when I talk about them openly, give me, give all of us, a unique opportunity to make a deep connection with others. These are the things that give me strength. Talking with other women, in particular, I found this is something we share. And some men relate to this too. Our levels of self-doubt can feel overwhelming at times but, when we share them, tough as that feels in the moment, when we name our fears, we find unexpected levels of connection and support.

For me the fear of making mistakes in learning our language continues to be a big one. My indigenous language, the language of my blood, of my heart, the language of *aroha* was something I have had to work hard at, to cry over, to feel miserable in failing at. I feared never being able to be fully fluent. And yet, I have learned to get over myself. To feel the fear and do it anyway. To step over the trap of self-indulgent self-criticism. To simply try again, and again. Where does this strength and courage come from?

In my *te reo Māori* (Māori language) journey I have learned that the emotions are expressed differently in our culture. *Hopo* is an emotion that does not translate directly into English – it means fear, trepidation, a sinking feeling of dread. It makes me reflect on the myriad of different ways that cultures express feelings and how much of these delicate nuances are lost when we only reference our emotions in English. Adding to our collective vocabulary of emotional words expands our experience of what is it to be human.

As a psychiatrist I am fascinated by the richness of expressing emotions in my culture. For example, we have many words for types of anxiety. Some of these start with the word *manawa*, a word for heart. So for us, some forms of anxiety are seen as a disruption of the heart. This is not too surprising given that anxiety can cause the heart to race, to pound, to flutter. Our English word, anxiety, doesn't directly link to this awareness anymore. What is truly transformative is that when I have used my cultural awareness of these Māori words with non-Māori patients as a way to consider their experience through a different lens, they have told me they find this very helpful in linking so directly with their feelings in the body.

Using our languages' creative ways of communicating our feelings adds another dimension to sharing our humanity. It helps to relieve the imposter syndrome because we can all draw on our innate cultural perspectives and words that give deeper insight into who we are.

*Tūwhitia te hopo* this week. Be brave and share some aspect of your culture as a gentle way to be closer to another human being and see how this can open up possibilities for letting go of fears.

# 2

# He iti hoki te mokoroa nāna i kakati te kahikatea.

While the mokoroa grub is small, it cuts through the white pine.

**There is power in small things.**

I can picture my ancestors observing the slow, steady tunnelling of this tiny grub, the *mokoroa*, slowly but surely eroding the mighty *kahikatea*, the white pine. It must have been dramatic to watch these magnificent trees fall, crashing to the forest floor, all because of a tiny, seemingly insignificant grub. They could respect the message of needing to attend to small details which, left unchecked, might destroy important aspects of life.

This *whakataukī* was brought into focus for me recently when I had to get my appendix removed. A strange, little part of the body, but suddenly rather important.

Ignoring my body's previous signals (we are all in danger of that, right?), I woke with a strange pain in the right-hand side of my stomach. Needless to say, I had acute appendicitis and the small, previously ignored bit of my bowel needed to come out.

I'm not afraid to say I was scared. I was scared about what they might find when they looked inside. I cried – in fear, in relief, in pain, in feeling loved, in feeling alone, in fear of death. This *whakataukī* makes me think about my little appendix having the potential to cut me down.

It really had me thinking about the little things that we can and should remove from our lives, which might appear insignificant but can, in fact, set in motion a cascade of events that can be negatively life-changing.

Sometimes we need to see that how we think, feel, the patterns we form and live by, are no longer healthy and we need to let them go. Sometimes these little bits of our thinking and behaviour have grown to damage us from within.

I wonder how to catch the *mokoroa* of my own thoughts, the negative thoughts and routines that burrow away? One thing I do every night before I fall asleep is to *mihi*, to acknowledge the day I have had. What does that mean? It is my way of practising gratitude, to salute the day and all of its offerings, no matter the ups and downs. I accept it all and the lessons the day gave me. This simple practice seems to make negative thoughts disappear into the night. I imagine them like the grubs, maturing into moths and fluttering up towards the stars. Using the imagination is something we do naturally as kids, but somehow we forget the power of our imaginations with age. I remind myself to draw on that creativity anytime and use the images from the *whakataukī* to strengthen the *aroha* of their messages. Try using your imagination to send negative thoughts away, let them sail away, float away, fly away from your mind. If drawing or writing are your thing, draw the thoughts and write about them leaving. Say goodbye to them and let them say goodbye to you.

# 3

# Poipoia te kākano kia puāwai.

## Nurture the seed and it will bloom.

**We all need love and care to fully realise our potential.**

The vitality so visible in the life of plants was an aspect keenly observed by our old people. I often wonder what it must have been like to walk in *te wao tapu nui a Tāne*, the sacred forests of Tāne when our ancestors first set foot in Aotearoa, New Zealand. A new climate, novel and unfamiliar plants. The awe in witnessing those seeds falling on the fertile ground, and how across seasons, rain and sun and the shelter of the family of other plants would see the steady growth of tiny sprouting shoots; the recognition of the ecological relationships that nurtured seeds into maturity and then to blossom.

Nurturing people according to nature's inherent instructions was natural for our ancestors. I have been told that back in the day the elders would watch the children and observe their inherent traits. Some were more confident by the water, with a knack for fishing; others rather quiet, preferring their own company in the dense silence of the forest or sitting beside their grandparents listening to stories; others, with beautiful singing voices and elegant movements. All the children would be nurtured according to their strengths. The quiet ones perhaps becoming carvers, the ones in tune with the sea being taught more about navigation, fishing and diving, the quick wits and good singers valued for their ability to entertain.

Nurturing ourselves is a struggle. I for one am not used to reaching out and letting people know I am not well, or even tired. Do you find that too? To be honest, I prefer to be the one looking after other people – that gives me great pleasure. And yet, lately I have been experimenting with the seed of more honest communication because I have been exhausted. I can feel that I have been running on empty. I need to take some of my own medicine.

What tends to happen more often in our lives is the '"How are you?" "I'm fine."' dance. We all buy into the 'busy' equals 'I am of value' principle of life; and the unspoken code that I'm too 'busy' to be anything other than fine and you are too 'busy' to listen, so what's the point in sharing anything real? We are all highly proficient at this.

It is much simpler when we have visibly healing physical wounds to prove our state of recovery, isn't it?

How uncaring our society can be towards people who are healing and recovering without external markings. People going through and healing from mental and emotional pain still remain largely unnoticed. And worse, we stick to our social codes that require silence.

We are a long, long way from building caring communities where people feel safe to talk openly with listeners who are truly hearing. Members of my *whānau* (extended family) and my patients have said to me over the years 'I don't want to talk to my friends about this', 'People will think I'm crazy', 'If people think you're crazy you may as well be dead', 'People will think I'm weak', 'They won't want to hang out with me anymore', 'I can't face the rejection', 'I need to just buck up', 'I have to keep this a secret'.

We are excellent at teaching ourselves to feel shame around any speaking out with any suggestion of mental health or addiction. Shame is a feeling of humiliation of the self, it is the 'I am bad.' As opposed to guilt, where the focus is on doing something bad. Shame is toxic as hell.

What can we do to unlearn shame in ourselves and unteach it in each other?

How can we simply be different from each other and accept these differences?

What gets in the way of being honest with ourselves and those we want to be closer to?

I am growing my honesty seeds and practising saying, 'I'm tired', 'I'm a bit overwhelmed, to be honest', 'I'm feeling sad', 'I'm feeling cross' – they seem to be the easier ones for me. My own honesty seeds are recognising there is fear in being vulnerable and allowing others to see when I am feeling life's burdens. And let's get real, life is not all plain sailing, so why perpetuate the idea that this might even come close to being my reality?

What am I afraid of? Why the 'best behaviour'?
I am taking more time to listen, to talk with my
nearest and dearest and to practice this honesty. It
is remarkable, it does get easier.

How we nurture our own seeds of truth is deeply
personal. Growth takes time, so make time to enable
those tender new shoots in our conversations to
flourish. Be more gentle with yourself because
this is unfamiliar territory, but there is so much
to be gained from building better and deeper
relationships with ourselves and then, through that
inner relationship, with the people in our lives.

# 4

# Ko te mauri, he mea huna ki te moana.

## The life force is hidden in the sea.

**Powerful aspects of life are hidden in plain sight.**

This *whakataukī* stems from one of our famous ancestors from the north, Nukutawhiti. He cast his *kura*, his feathered cloak, into the Hokianga Harbour to calm the waters for safe passage. And this treasure remains there, out of sight, yet signifies the ancient presence of those that have gone before.

This saying has given me strength so many times. I have always found it comforting because it speaks to the hidden magic of life.

It reminds me of those things we feel intuitively but often ignore – we can choose to tune in to our gut instinct, for example, or wait until the messages become clearer and more obvious.

And it reminds me that we all have hidden powers inside us that we can too easily forget. Lately I have been thinking about this *whakataukī* in relation to my *moko kauae*, the facial markings I have worn since Matariki, the Māori new year, 17 June, 2017. I have always been fascinated by *moko kauae*. As a child, I looked in wonder at pictures of the women with these scarifications. I remember thinking that mine was hidden under the surface of my skin and would one day appear, as if by magic.

Growing up, I heard so many different things about what it meant to be eligible to wear *moko kauae*. I heard that you had to be an expert speaker of our language, you must uphold our cultural values and it was necessary to be shoulder-tapped as ready for this honour. I have mulled this over for many years, speaking to my relations and friends who had already taken that step. One of my esteemed female friends, who has carried the *moko kauae* for many years, asked me one day, 'What are you waiting for?' So, I gave her a list of my inadequacies: I was not fluent enough, I hadn't achieved enough in my work. She looked me right in the eye and said, 'So?'

And, in fact, deep down, hidden under those layers, I knew in my gut that the time was right. Maybe the fact that we were having the conversation over the water made a difference too. I was suddenly aware of the hidden, treasured feather cloak deep under the waves, like the *moko kauae* under my skin.

And so my own *moko kauae*, once obscured from view, was revealed. People ask me if it hurt. It didn't. *Karakia*, prayers, took me into a meditative realm. I would occasionally surface to hear the talking and singing of those around me and then I would float away again. I recall being under the ocean at one point. Swimming in deep waters, feeling the gentle water against my body. An overwhelming sense of calm. A powerful sense of coming home.

This *whakataukī* is part of my *moko kauae* story. It is a reminder that so much of our lives' achievements can be hidden from us. That we can forget our powers, and what we contribute to the world, when the ancient resources are hard to see.

Reclaim your childhood memories – recall them. Bring forward with your mind the simple truths and hopes that you connected with when you were young and that growing up somehow made you dismiss as 'childish'. Maybe start with something simple like washing your face. It might sound strange, but whether you like a cold splash or a gentle warm flannel, this simple act can help to bring your attention in those moments to an act of kindness for yourself. In those few seconds just let any positive memories of childhood emerge. Maybe these will give you some clues to follow in discovering more about how to bring forward some uplifting aspects of yourself.

Remember your hidden powers, your true self, and bring it into the light.

# 5

# He ihu kurī, he tangata haere.

As a dog follows a scent, a traveller relies on the hospitality of others.

**Beware blindly following your nose. Be deliberate, make good choices.**

I have been pondering this *whakataukī* while doing some good, hard looking in the mirror.

The *whakataukī* helps to remind me to be aware of the difference between doing something mindlessly, as a habit that might not be best for me, and doing something intentionally, thoughtfully and making the smarter choice. You can apply this to all kinds of things, including relationships where harmful patterns can easily emerge when your heart can overrule your head.

This *whakataukī* reminds us to seek real hospitality for yourself, within your own heart, with your own *aroha*, and warns of the dangers of following what is not real through force of habit or the thrill of the rush of adrenaline when we meet someone exciting.

This proverb reminds me that there are primitive forces, certain scents that some of us subconsciously lock onto. Perhaps those pheromones are part of what ignites certain responses, a sudden oxytocin flood to the brain. Like Pavlov's dog, perhaps we find ourselves conditioned to lay out the welcome mat all too often and invite a negative relationship into our lives? This is where our *whānau* (family) can support us and help us see repeated behaviours. Maybe the *whakataukī* can be the alert you need for an environmental scan of relationships – to check in, with *aroha*, and be clear about decisions of the heart.

# 6

# Ko Atutahi te whetū tārake o te rangi.

## Canopus is visible out in the open expanse of the sky.

**An outstanding individual.**

When I think of truly outstanding people in my life I keep coming back to my teachers. I can't help feeling I have been supremely lucky with them all. I remember my piano teacher, Miss Rodway. Always smiling, patient at my mistakes and lack of practice. All those jarring off-key notes. She never flinched. So enthusiastic with that essence of 'teacher-joy' that spills over and fills you up with a warm glow. Mrs Tomlinson, my English teacher, she had great nails too I recall – even length, perfect moons, never wore nail polish. She created a vivid world where English grammar was fun – I know, how is that even possible, right? Mrs Mitchinson, drama teacher extraordinaire, daring, witty and outrageous – we all wanted to be her. And then my teachers at medical school, so many fizzing with excitement about their fields of research and practice! Perhaps Professor Sir Richard Faull has been the most influential. He became one of my PhD supervisors, part of my post doctoral research support team and then my boss. Every meeting, every event, a masterclass in how to share the love of learning and discovery.

The group of teachers that have truly captured my heart and are now intertwined with my DNA are my *te reo Māori* (Māori language) teachers. It is hard to find words for these *mumu reo*, these language warriors. They fight for the survival of our language. They get up every morning and do it again and again every day. They are relentless. The epitome of perseverance. And they are so much fun. Even the ones who have a veneer of the grumpy about them, have their mischievious side too. They have that loving irritation that stems from the urgency. The urgency required for us to learn, to speak with our Māori tongues and listen with our Māori hearts and speak our language with Māori minds, with a return to the values of our ancestors.

Of course, our language is changing as all languages do. Our *rangatahi*, our young people text in te reo. KTK (*kino te katakata*) is our LOL (laugh out loud). This has become so common that some of us older ones use KTK too. I remember someone saying to me once that, 'Of course there is no Māori word for coffee machine, because you didn't have one of those on the *waka* (canoe) when you arrived here.' Such a strange idea, that the Māori language would not evolve to develop words for emerging technology. Every language in the world has had to adapt and evolve across millennia. I was able to reassure the person that indeed we do have such words. A coffee machine, by the way, can be called a *kutētē*, reminiscent of a machine used to milk cows. We also have words for computer (*rorohiko*, literally electric brain), leggings (*tarau piri hākinakina*, close-fitting sports pants) and the immune system (*pūnaha awhikiri*).

There is always that one teacher that you wanted to impress, right? I am the same. And for me this is the teacher where I made the most classic, dumb mistakes. Literally those slap-your-forehead moments where you want the ground to swallow you up. We were chatting during a break in class and I said, 'He tamariki koe?' Literally, 'Are you a child?' What I meant to say was, 'He tamariki āu?', 'Do you have children?' As clangers go, that was right up there. As soon as the words left my mouth I knew I had screwed up. I recall a subtle sigh and exhale from him. But in true, top-teacher form he just rolled on with the correct sentence. I still cringe a bit when I think of it. But hey, I won't make that particular mistake again. It's true what they say – it's how people make you feel – and great teachers have a way of supporting and cajoling that learning along with their *aroha*, their deep love for students, their learning and the *kaupapa*, the subject, in this case the life blood of our culture, our language. Truly, they are the stars that illuminate our learning paths by shining light into the parts of ourselves we cannot see. When I am in the thick of learning I know I can easily get bogged down in all the things I feel I am getting wrong, all the mistakes, and these inspirational teachers keep shining that light, no matter what. Atutahi is the Māori name for Canopus, one of the brightest stars in the sky. And so, just like Atutahi, my teachers continue to make my path twinkle with their brilliance. I wonder who your outstanding teachers have been? And how do we continue to honour all their efforts?

# 7

# E koekoe te tūī, e ketekete te kākā, e kūkū te kererū.

The tūī squawks, the kākā chatters, the kererū coos.

**It takes all kinds of people.**

I love the abundance of native birds in the bush where I live. Since the neighbourhood put in place a rat eradication programme, we have all noticed a huge growth in the bird population. The birds are returning in greater and greater numbers now that the introduced predators are being systematically removed from the ecosystem. We still have some rats, stoats and ferrets but eventually these will all be gone. Our feathered friends will once again be free from these attacks on their eggs and young.

The variety of our birds is astonishing. They all have different ways of communicating, different plumage, different ways of life. Our ancestors took great heed of the birds. They interpreted the signs birds conveyed in ways that have, to a great extent, been lost in today's world. They left *whakataukī* to give us some clues about the many lessons we can receive from observing birdlife.

The differences amongst the birds are so clear, their calls perhaps most especially. The way they communicate, their language. This was very meaningful to our ancestors. The bird call can be thought of as the bird's identity. And so this proverb is about acceptance and non-judgment. We have many differences, the way we speak, the way we look, the way we live and we are at the same time all humans. And yet there are times when we are so focussed on our differences. And this can cause so much pain and suffering. How can we be more like birds, co-existing in the bush? Diversity is normal to them, not just a word in policy documents. In fact, one bird, the *pīpīwharauroa* (shining cuckoo), lays its egg in another bird's nest, that of the *riroriro* (grey warbler). This tiny bird raises the baby *pīpīwharauroa* alongside its own chicks.

How could you take this invitation from our old people to bring acceptance and non-judgment into your daily life, like our native birds? When do you notice judgment starting to creep into your day? Is it when you are tired or stressed or do you have some people you hold certain judgmental ideas about? How could you shift those patterns? Maybe watch some birds today and imagine yourself flying free of the judgment you experience from others? This might help you to let go of your non-acceptance, because you know how much judgment and non-acceptance hurts.

# 8

# E ngaki ana a mua, e tōtō mai ana a muri.

First clear the weeds, then plant.

**Make time for mind-weeding.**

*Wairua* is the Māori concept of being connected to everything in the universe, also translated sometimes as spirituality. Just like the *māra* (garden), the mind-body-*wairua* (spirit) system requires regular weeding. No one actually teaches us to gently and kindly examine the thoughts and feelings that we internalise that are not really ours. But it is such an important practice, because otherwise we can unwittingly internalise these thoughts and feelings and they can become integrated into our consciousness.

For me this *whakataukī* is so poignant because I have been taking time to clear out the detritus in my own head, reflecting on what is most important, what my legacy is as a parent, as *whānau* (family), what I want to contribute to the world around me.

When I finished medical school I did a kind of full mind-body-*wairua* scan in order to shed values and ideas that were not healthy for me. Things like, 'Māori doctors are not as good as non-Māori doctors', 'Māori services are less skilled', 'Because you are Māori you will never be a success.' While these values and ideas were not explicitly expressed to me during my training, marginalising and racist ideas were implicitly conveyed to me and my peers. One of the things I witnessed as a by-product of this implicit messaging was Māori putting down other Māori. It's a brilliant colonising tool used throughout history – to get the colonised to bring themselves down. It has a name, lateral violence, and it does just that, it violates and hurts others.

Regular weeding of such damaging ideas is essential if we are to remain healthy and clear in our vision of a resourceful, self-determined future for our *whānau*.

Whenever I think of this *whakataukī* I am also mindful of the phases of the moon. For our ancestors, timing, according to the moon, was vital. Every night, every moon phase has its own name. There is a specific time for planting, a time for harvesting, and a time for weeding. There are periods of the lunar cycle where the impact on people's energy and mood is anticipated. For example, you need energy for weeding and you need to be sure you are focussed, otherwise you can end up pulling out everything, not only weeds. So you need to pick the right times of the month, literally.

Our minds inherently require a clearing of space to prepare for the planting of new seeds. These ideas are not new. It is ancient, time-honoured wisdom that kept our ancestors healthy and in tune with the natural world. We need now, more than ever, to stay grounded and to stay connected to the wisdom of the past. Uproot your mind-weeds and plant that positive-knowledge legacy.

You might ask how to start doing this. Recognise the times of the day and the month when you feel at your best, energised. Look up at the moon. How do you feel? Schedule in some time when you feel ready to get a little mind-weeding done.

# 9

# He kokonga whare e kitea; he kokonga ngākau e kore e kitea.

The corners of a house may be seen and examined; not so the corners of the heart.

**The heart holds many secrets.**

I have always been intrigued by this *whakataukī*. It is heard in welcomes and in intimate gatherings so, like all *whakataukī*, it has a wide breadth of meaning, depending on the context. In the *whaikōrero*, the formal speeches at gatherings, eloquent speakers use this *whakataukī*. It emphasises the seen and the hidden. It reminds us that there are layers of overt and covert and that some things are extremely powerful but not spoken of, yet nevertheless continue to influence our actions.

The recesses of the heart hide so much. When I think of the corners of my own heart, there are many stories and names and scars. There are experiences, bruises and unfulfilled hopes in my heart which I may never speak of again.

It is said that if one woman told the truth about her life, the world would split open. It feels like our world may already be splitting open and maybe that is why we often keep our own counsel, but the world needs to be opened up to the reality of the secrets of our hearts. Even though it feels relatively unsafe to talk, we are compelled to.

One striking example for me is our experiences of our fertility, the loss of pregnancies, of not becoming pregnant, of complications during pregnancy and delivery, of mental illness during and after pregnancy – these are all massive areas of mostly unspoken grief. I am shocked when I find medical colleagues who gloss over these experiences with *whānau*, extended family, – who carry these losses in their own ways. All genders carry these issues. Grief is often kept tightly private in an attempt to protect others. Other times it spills out in overwhelming ways. I am privileged to work with *whānau* who go through such trials.

There is so much pain and anguish involved with the loss of pregnancy and the struggles of people who want to have a baby. These stories are so deeply personal and intimate that many take them to the grave.

Perhaps one of the strengths in our Māori community is our ability to come together and support our young parents and their experiences of pregnancy. Back in the day I worked to provide some care at Teen Parenting units in South Auckland schools. One of the things I recall vividly is the strength and the courage of our young parents and their ability to rapidly learn new skills. Let's not fall into the trap of thinking our young parents can't do the job. They absolutely can. And they need our support.

So the corners of our hearts hide our deepest secrets and fears, our grief and loss. Many of these stories may never be told and we come to accept this as reality. What are some truths we can begin to tell? How can we find avenues where it is safe to reveal those hidden heart spaces, at the very least to shed light for future generations?

# 10

# E ea ai te werawera o Tāne tahuaroa, me heke te werawera o Tāne te wānanga.

Satisfy the sweat of the cooks by getting a good sweat up while learning.

**To properly acknowledge the efforts of the cooks, we need to give learning our all.**

Food and hospitality are at the heart of showing care and respect for others. They are activities that demonstrate *aroha*, our love for others. This is at the core of our identity. We call this value *manaakitanga*.

This *whakataukī* is often used at *wānanga*, gatherings, many of which are for the purpose of learning. I have attended a number of total immersion *wānanga* over the years where the aim is to grow people's command of our language, *te reo Māori*. It is common practice for a member of the visitor group to stand and make a speech at the end of the final meal of the *wānanga*, thanking the cooks for their efforts. These speeches usually find some way to link the *werawera*, the sweat, and hard work of the kitchen, all those involved with running the *wānanga*, with the students, recognising that their commitment to their learning is a way of honouring those who make the food. This proverb is one of the favourites for that setting. We often joke that no matter the quality of the *wānanga*, if the food was poor or insufficient the whole *wānanga* is remembered for that alone. This would be a black mark against all involved in organising that gathering.

For me this *whakataukī* highlights the importance of putting into practice the mutuality of responsibilities in our lives. Our efforts must be linked and not seen or experienced in isolation. In some cultures the efforts of those who prepare our food remain undervalued or even ignored. Making food with love and attention is a truly beautiful gift. I learned this from my mum. She was a great cook. She could rustle up scones for visitors at a moment's notice. She was a dab hand at any kind of roast as well as Italian and Indian cuisine. She passed many of her skills on to me, and I have passed these on to my kids who are both very skilled in the kitchen. I have been very lucky at different times when my son came home to live as an adult and would cook if I was working late. Best lasagne ever.

In our *whānau* (family) home I have passed on the sentiment that hard work of any kind, but especially learning, and sharing meals, is a perfect way to honour those who prepared the food. Plus it makes for great meal-time conversation. Sitting down together to eat is such an important part of family life and it is being eroded by the use of devices. Having a period where devices are off for meals is crucial. I have been guilty of having my phone nearby when we are eating and then being called out by my kids. Quite rightly. When I cook for the family I really appreciate hearing about the day's learnings, which does make me feel that my time has been honoured. What can we do more of in our households to honour those who prepare the food? How can we create time and space to honour each other's roles and responsibilities? How can that shared and reciprocal nourishment of both food and relationships be recognised and celebrated?

# 11

# Ko Hinemoa, ko ahau.

I am just like Hinemoa;
I'd risk all for love.

**Love has no guarantees.**

It is a big responsibility carrying the same name
as a famous Māori woman. And someone from a
different *iwi* (tribe). And someone who is named in
a *whakataukī*, about love.

Hinemoa, the original, came from a small village
on the shores of lake Rotorua. She and a young man
called Tūtanekai from Mokoia, the island in the
middle of the lake, fell in love. The *whānau* (family)
were none too happy about this. So Tūtanekai, back
on the island, played his flute across the water to

her every night to let her know he was thinking of her. Eventually she couldn't take it anymore and swam across the lake. She hid in a hot pool and pretended to be a *taniwha* (water spirit) to frighten Tūtanekai's water-bearer. When Tūtanekai came to see what was going on, Hinemoa revealed herself to him. Long story short, they ended up together and produced many descendants who live on today in their *papa kāinga* (original home) and around the world. The *wharenui* (meeting house), named Tūtanekai and the *wharekai* (dining hall), named Hinemoa, stand as sentinels to these *tūpuna* (ancestors) in the exquisite setting of Ōwhata.

Hinemoa took a big risk in swimming across the lake. She risked the anger and rejection of her *whānau*.

This *whakataukī* reminds us that love is all about risk. Love has no guarantees. Love requires a massive leap of faith. I have made that leap a few times in my life.

Like the waters rippling on lake Rotorua, love must feel free and unconstrained. If I should ever take that leap again, I will try to hold onto that. 'Try' being the operative word, because that is the other thing love does, it throws everything you think you have learned out the window.

# 12

# Ehara! Ko koe te ringa e huti punga!

## Yes, yours is the arm best suited to pull up the anchor!

**You have it in you!**

Giving praise is something we can all do more of. This *whakataukī* highlights an important skill – to take notice, to pay attention and to describe the good things you see others doing. Pulling up the anchor on a *waka*, a canoe or boat, is not an easy task. Most often the anchors were massive, heavy stones. Pulling up the anchor is also not something that you can bail out of half-way and decide, this is not the right time. It requires spiritual, physical and mental strength. Pulling up anchors in times gone by involved invocations to the spiritual realm. It is also an action that has to happen at a certain time of the tide to ensure the safety of the vessel. You have to see it through to the end. So, you get the picture that the person who takes responsibility for this is vital to the journey.

I love to picture our ancestors on their ocean-going *waka*. Their supreme skills with every part of the *waka* that carried them across Te Moana-nui-a-Kiwa, the Pacific Ocean. Their strength, their courage. I see them pulling up the anchor and setting sail for new adventures, in harmony with the natural world.

*Waka* in our culture are symbols of many things – the family, our language, our *whakapapa* (genealogy). Pulling up the anchor also happens at a particular stage, when a period of being settled at anchor is over and the *waka* is beginning a new journey. So a person who enables the timely departure of a *waka* is to be relied upon. These words of powerful encouragement are truly empowering. Many times, people in our lives who are the ones who continue to pull up the anchor – the strong, responsive, reliable ones – get little reward. They do not necessarily have an obvious status within *whānau* (family), but they are vital to our lives' journeys.

What fascinates me is that we can be that for ourselves. We must be able to rely on ourselves to up anchor and open a new chapter. I remind myself that I have done this a few times in my life. Ending a relationship where I had been in denial about our mutual unhappiness was one such up-anchor moment. It took me a while to realise it was up to me to pull up the anchor of my own *waka*. And it was very painful. Maybe you have done this for yourself too? It sometimes seems easier to stay settled in a particular place in our lives. How can we get better at recognising when it is time to be our own change agents? How much distress do we need to be in before we make the decision to embrace a new voyage and pull up that anchor?

# 13

# Aroha mai, aroha atu.

## Love received demands love returned.

**Love others and love will come back to you.**

I have made a commitment to record moments of deep connection and passionate joy, every day for the next twelve months.

This *whakataukī* speaks to me about receiving love and creating a deliberate daily practice to remind myself of the energy of this love every day. I realised I had retreated to the cave of work. I had ensured that all of my time was devoted to the many contributions I felt compelled to be involved with.

Maybe you can relate? I wanted to make sure I was responsive to the multiple needs of my extended family and community. And at a certain level this was my way of avoiding a deep level of connection with my own heart. This was diminishing my inner wellspring of *aroha* and I could begin to feel that I was running on empty.

I started recording memories of these precious moments. The sunshine dancing on the waves, the purity of the white snow, the intense, inspiring eye contact of a friend, the warmth of a hug. I am now a collector of these moments. These are my own moments of noticing *aroha* all around me. Already this is proving an extraordinary exercise. So exquisitely nourishing. I am more and more aware of all the aspects of *aroha* surrounding me. Fuelling my passion for living, my joy, the importance of deep connection to feeding my soul. One of the unexpected consequences is that I feel such freedom. A weight lifted. I can feel this *aroha* effect in my lightness of being, in my ready smile. This is the effervescence of *aroha* as it spills out into all the nooks and crannies of my life where little shadows of loneliness and grief hid. I invite you to try this on for size. See how the *aroha* effect works for you.

# Kaitiakitanga

### Te aroha ki
### a Papatūānuku

**Taking care** of our planet, our earth mother, our oceans, waterways and forests was once at the heart of our well being. Our unique identity as guardians was the source of the restorative cycle of *aroha* in our lives. As caretakers we valued this caring relationship between ourselves and our natural environment, and this attitude, these skills and knowledge defined us. These days, the catastrophic rifts in our guardianship role, our estrangement from this critical part of who we intrinsically are is harming us every day. The challenge to reclaim this *aroha* is at the heart of many *whakataukī*. They guide us back to this way of living more contented lives. This aspect of *aroha*, the activation of our role as custodians is at the heart of our very survival and that of our mother earth, Papatūānuku.

# 14

# E kore tātau e mōhio ki te waitohu nui o te wai kia mimiti rawa te puna.

We never know the worth of water until the well runs dry.

**Look after the planet before it is too late.**

Te Wharehuia Milroy

This *whakatauākī* is very special. It was coined by arguably our greatest teacher of *whakataukī* of modern times, Te Wharehuia Milroy. He was a professor, a leader, a teacher of *te reo Māori* (Māori language) to many of us who attended *kura reo*, total immersion learning retreats. He was an inspiration who challenged us to go forth and speak our language and share the wisdom of our culture with pride. I am one of the lucky ones to have been taught by him – and to have experienced his cheeky laugh, his twinkling eyes and his deep wisdom. He called us the '*puananī*', the seeds of the dandelion clock blown by the winds, because we have the responsibility of spreading our language and culture far and wide.

Central to Māori beliefs is that our connection to mother earth is essential to our own wellbeing. Because of that the distress of our planet hurts us too. Perhaps it is only now, with the realisation that our planet is in such deep trouble, that we can also recognise our own well 'running dry'. We are frail when our world is fragile. We have a reciprocal relationship with mother earth.

Reports about global warming have made me think in a new way about how we consider ourselves and our community. Most scientists now agree that climate change is real, human activity is the cause (how we live, how we make things, our use of non-renewable resources like oil, gas and coal, our reliance on cars, deforestation . . .), and we are heating up the planet at a destructive rate.

Islands in the western Pacific are already under water. Our precious ecosystems of animals, insects, birds, fish are all being impacted, as are we.

How are these changing environmental conditions impacting our health?

For one thing, our kids and grandkids are anxious about the future, and quite rightly. How do we reassure them, with any honesty, when we know the future is precarious?

For our own personal wellbeing we must restore harmony to our environment. Not using single-use plastics, planting more trees, lobbying our governments and industries to reduce emissions, for example, are not just good acts for our world, but good acts for us personally too. Being more aware, kinder, more open, more loving towards our environment and the people, animals and things that co-exist alongside us, will help us tune in to how our environment impacts us – weather, seasons, our surroundings.

How does it all make you feel? Are there things you can change to make your own life more positive and look after your little patch of the world too?

I live in a community where we rely on rain water in our homes. It changes your relationship with water very quickly. No running the tap when you brush your teeth. Visitors from the city learn to adapt pretty quickly. When we have droughts the tank can run dry. Then we have to buy water delivered from the aquifer. Living like this for more than 20 years evokes a highly respectful relationship with water. The scarcity of water is a daily reality that is becoming more and more common all over the world.

One thing I do is to make sure I am close to the ocean, a river or a lake as often as possible. I take some time to pick up any rubbish I find. I think about how clean the water is and what we might do to make that body of water in that specific area cleaner. Wherever I can I try to get into the water, even if it's just my feet or to splash a little water onto my face and head and to give thanks for all that water gives us. Let's take those opportunities to value water, both physically and metaphorically to prevent the well running completely dry of all the waters that keep us alive.

# 15

# Me te wai kōrari.

Like the nectar of the flax flower.

**Joy in small things.**

I love to watch *tūī* (parson birds) around my home dipping their beaks into the elegant champagne flutes of the *harakeke* (flax) flowers. The flax bushes send up magnificent regal stems of flowers in the summer and the *tūī* gorge themselves on the sweet nectar. They often wear a sprinkling of the pollen on their foreheads, a clear sign of their persistence in reaching deep into the floral cups.

It is a signal of nature's abundance and the connectivity of life. Watching the birds makes my heart feel so full, makes me glad to be alive to witness this simple, delicious pleasure.

This *whakataukī* is a reminder from our ancestors to take time to notice such beauty. *Tūī* have mellifluous voices. Beautiful singers are likened to them – *he korokoro tūī* is said of a person who can really sing. Throughout the valley they sing at the top of their lungs. I imagine them singing in the days of our ancestors. They sing to me of those days of deep understanding of the place of humans in the natural world. A time of humility, when humans were respectful of nature and in tune with it. We have come a long way and made extraordinary advances, there is no doubt. But what have we sacrificed? The song of the *tūī* and their summer dance on the *harakeke*, quaffing that exquisite honey water calls to me to live the dreams of our forebears. To find ways to take care of the planet every day with small, careful steps.

To celebrate the life we have. To be aware of actions that work against our being alive, not for it. To deliberately choose to protect and preserve our natural world.

What is it that gives you joy? How could you celebrate being alive and being part of nature? In looking out the window, in talking to a small child, in letting the leaves of a plant touch your skin? How can you let nature touch you today?

# 16

# Ka tū tonu koe i roto i te aroha.

## Stand in the love.

**Be true to the love within you.**

Whaea Moe Milne

Pārengarenga is the ocean, Waimirirangi is my ancestor, Tawhitirahi is the mountain, Awapoka the river, Pōtahi is one of my marae – these are my tribal affiliations and this is the *aroha* I stand in.

You may wonder, what is the point of that introduction? It is a *pepeha*, a greeting. You saw it at the beginning of this book. It locates me in time and space according to the places of my ancestors and their stories. It grounds me and it weaves together multiple layers through which we Māori see connections between us. *Pepeha* are increasingly used by non-Māori too. In this way, who I am, the important aspects that make up my identity are made visible to you. That is the purpose of *pepeha* – building relationships. Our lands, seas, mountains, rivers, lakes are so powerfully, so tangibly part of our identities here in Aotearoa, New Zealand. When we say the names of our places we can instantly be transported there, to those places and their stories, we can be in those memories, and this is part of how we know who we are. Such is the power of our minds.

Whaea Moe Milne, one of my esteemed female mentors and guides through my life and career coined this *whakatauākī* when we were working together to develop a *kaupapa Māori* (by Māori, for Māori) child and adolescent mental health team. She taught me that when I am reciting my *pepeha* I need to see and feel myself in those places that I speak of. I must stand on my mountain, be in my ocean, my river, be in my meeting house and be with my ancestors. For me, this links so intimately with her other teaching about standing in the love. Because this is how we can experience the *aroha* that emanates from the land, from the sea, from our mother earth.

*Aroha* is a divine feeling. It is strong and it is never-ending. It comes up out of the ground. We feel it in the warmth of our *marae* (traditional meeting places), and with our ancestors, in the places they walked, swam, loved. This ancient love is tangible. We breathe it. We activate and reinvigorate it when we use our *pepeha*.

This is not the exclusive domain of Māori. All ethnic groups have traditions that ground peoples and places together. What I love is that we Māori have this potent, time-honoured tradition of *pepeha*, which makes our identity very clear. What *pepeha* does is firmly lays down a kind of welcome mat on which we can then discover how we are connected through the stories and peoples of our lands, across Aotearoa and the world.

I have a vivid memory of a *whānau* (family) reunion at Ahipara. I can picture the beach of my youth in my mind. My eye balls stretching to take it all in. The thumping of the waves, the light shimmering on the water, blinding. I can feel the sand under my toes, soft and scrunchy and I can see the imprint of my feet as I retrace my steps back to my laughing relations.

Going back to that childhood memory makes me smile. It has that primordial pull. And there is more than a tinge of sadness. I think about my mum in the same moment, she's sitting next to me. My mum who gave me this connection to that laughter, that beach, that ocean. She didn't speak *te reo Māori* (Māori language), she was part of those generations where 'being Māori' was actively discouraged, sometimes with violence. This hurt her. She cried about it.

I see the same pain in the eyes of the young people, many of whom are my *whanaunga*, my relations, who I see for assessments when I write court reports. They often tell me, jokingly 'I'm a bit of a plastic Māori, I don't know where I'm from.' They can't tell me their mountain, their river, their places and their histories.

Their stories are waiting to be found, to be brought to life. If you don't know your story, seek it out. I have seen with my own eyes how powerful learning *pepeha* can be. The transformation when our *taiohi*, our young ones, learn their *pepeha* at the Kōti Rangatahi (youth court) held on *marae* (traditional meeting places). It gives me goosebumps thinking about it now. There is a squaring of the shoulders, a new, warm and confident eye contact, a sense of healthy identity, a sense of direction, if you will. A resetting of the cultural compass. And it's portable. They can now take that with them wherever they go. It's protective.

So you can probably picture me in those assessments when I'm meeting our *taiohi* in my role as court report writer. I'm unashamedly using the connections with my own *pepeha* and whatever I can glean about theirs. *Pepeha* work like a kind of uniting code – following clues, you can put into words the connections that bind us all together.

My experience has shown me that *pepeha* are the heart of, literally, a bringing home, to your self, to your own. Like I say, this is not the exclusive domain of Māori. How might you explore your own cultural traditions of places that are meaningful to you and your ancestors and bring that forward? How can you bring to life that intimate connection with the places of your forebears and harness that portable healthy identity? When you need strength, can you call to mind the lands in which you were born?

# 17

# Ehara i te aurukōwhao, he takerehāia!

## Not a leak in the upper lashings, but an open rent in the hull!

**Not a minor mishap, but rather a major catastrophe!**

We are in the middle of a major catastrophe. At the same time it feels like we are in a bizarre parallel universe where re-runs of the *Emperor's New Clothes* fairy tale are on rotate. A planet where everyone is pretending things are okay, when really we are so far from that. Where did we learn denial and minimisation and avoidance as a global community? How did we learn to tune out the deafening waves of information breaching our global *waka* (canoe)? Data clearly shows that we have truly screwed up our planet's ecosystems and we must take clear, decisive action to try to rescue the situation on behalf of generations to come.

Our ancestors use the metaphor of the *waka* over and over again because this is such a powerful image for the carriage of life itself. Having been through the Drake Passage twice on the way to and from the Antarctic Peninsula, I have had a tiny glimpse into the world of our ocean-going ancestors.

When will we start talking about what is happening to our planet in a way that the decision-makers take notice of and really make some clear decisions to put things right?

One of the issues that is very clear is that data alone is not going to sway the decision-makers, whoever they may be. Numbers are necessary but not sufficient. Just like telling people not to smoke, not to eat food that is unhealthy. Giving people factual information is important but it doesn't necessarily change how we behave. How bad does the situation have to get before you will do things differently?

You might have a meat-free day once a week, drive an electric vehicle, start a vegetable garden, conserve water? What are your stories about the imminent death of our planet? What do you care about? What actually matters to you? What is your line in the sand?

This week, write a letter to your grandchildren, or to local children who will be born in 2050, about what you did to stop the demise of our world, and when you started to change.

# 18

# Tama tū, tama ora; tama noho, tama mate.

He who stands, lives; he who does nothing, perishes.

**Just do it.**

I have recently spoken at a conference on pathways to resilience. It is an interesting word, resilience, and it gets bandied about a fair bit. In my work with patients recovering from brain injuries, one thing became clearly important in their recovery, in their ability to build resilience, and that was *wairua*. For resilience in life, we all need *wairua*.

*Wairua* is sometimes translated as spirituality or soul. There are *wairua*-strengthening practices we can all do: activities like *karakia* (incantations, prayers), *waiata* (songs and chants), being on marae (traditional meeting places) and speaking *te reo Māori* (Māori language). These are practices that foster our resilience.

You are likely familiar with the mighty New Zealand men's rugby team, the All Blacks, and the *haka* that begins every match they play? This iconic Māori cultural act is one clear way to create, signal and maintain resilience.

We now face the brutal impact of the abuse of Papatūānuku, mother earth, in a way that changes all of our lives forever. Our Māori *tikanga*, our cultural practices, of *karakia*, of *waiata*, of *haka*, and our *reo* offer us such potent resilience. These practices, uniquely rooted in our land, can play an integral part in our collective healing now and into the future.

For each one of us, if we are going to act with purpose from the heart, we need to take care of ourselves. We must stand up for our inner health and wellbeing first. It doesn't help the planet or each other if we are exhausted.

Saying a *karakia mō te kai* (prayer before food) is a simple way that our family takes a moment to breathe and slow down to express gratitude for our food. We use an ancient prayer that acknowledges the Māori deities of our earth mother, sky father, those that protect the oceans and gardens. It really brings us together and makes us stop and notice each other's presence and the delicious *kai* (food) before us. My hypothesis is that it is good for the digestion too. Someone needs to do that research, the impact of prayers before food on digestion and relaxation.

Give it a try. When your descendants ask you, 'What did you do to look after our world?' you can say you started by giving thanks for the abundance of our planet and the food it provides. Not a bad place to start.

# 19

# Me he Ōturu ngā karu.

Like the large eyes of a beautiful woman.

**True beauty can be seen in the eyes.**

Ōturu means full moon, beaming with luminescence and power. Our ancestors loved metaphors involving the celestial bodies, especially the moon. Life was arranged by a lunar calendar, so the moon had immense influence. And the moon for us is a female deity.

The moon is timeless, yet ever-changing as she moves through her cycles. There is great solace and courage to be drawn from her steady presence. We can look up in the night sky and always know she is there.

Even on nights when she is in darkness, when I might be feeling that gloom too, I know there will be increasing slivers of her beguiling light in the coming evenings. It gives me the sense of my own emerging lightness during the month. I look up and think of our female ancestors who also drew on the moon's lovely light as a reminder of the cycles of beauty that transcend age. The gentle fall of moonlight on our skin, our lips, our eyes – that is what epitomises true attraction and beauty first and foremost to ourselves. Our ancient wisdom provides the perfect antidote to the superficial ideals of contemporary beauty.

The female interstellar energy of this *whakataukī* speaks to me about ageing. As a woman in my fifties I am acutely aware of the enormous pressures to look young. The prevailing societal norm highlights that young is attractive, old is not. I was recently told by a complete stranger, 'You are still beautiful.' It was a slightly backhanded compliment, as if to suggest that at my age beauty is not to be expected. It makes me chuckle that people feel they can rock up and share comments about appearance. It is not the first time. I recall a female medical colleague who I barely knew once blurting out, 'Gosh, you have put on weight.' That ranks right up there with being told how 'brave' I was to end a relationship at 'your age' because 'you probably won't find anyone else now'. I had to mull that one over. So many elements of social control right there. The idea that some other people feel societal pressure to be in a relationship touches on a deeply felt fear of women who live without a partner, who are self-determining and who are fulfilled living according to their own plan. Our female ancestors had their own *mana* (status) and were not reliant on male partners for this. I am reminded of the words of one of our famous female leaders who marched to the beat of her own drum, quite literally, Dame Whina Cooper. She once said to me about my then husband, 'If he is not good to you, leave him.' I was a bit taken aback at the time. Now I look back and think how blessed I have been to have such straight-talking women around me.

Regardless of our gender, the external rules of beauty and the push towards those are a form of cruelty to us all and frankly against nature. We are all uniquely beautiful, like the moon in different phases, and our beauty is changing too. Our ancestors are inviting us to look to the constants of our environment, like our dreamy moon, and see ourselves in her allure.

# 20

Ko ō tātou
whakapono ngā
kaiwehewehe
i a tātau. Ko ō
tātau moemoeā
me ō tātau
pākatokato ngā
kaiwhakakotahi i a
tātau.

It is our truths that are the actors of separation. It is our dreams and difficulties that act to unify us.

**Ideologies separate us. Dreams and adversity bring us together.**

Te Wharehuia Milroy

We speak different languages, we have different histories and these separate us. These make us distinctive and unique. Our elders knew and respected this.

Our ancestors were also fundamentally concerned with survival. For that they needed some unity of purpose. Not much has changed across the generations. Our current climate emergency makes me think about this in a new way. We need to find ways to remain true to our differences and at the same time focus on making our dreams for a safe and healthy planet real. In fact, the breakthrough is discovering ways we can communicate both our local and global selves. The extent to which we can be unified through respecting and valuing our differences is the key.

This *whakatauākī* brings us back to the critical importance of this balance of identity. I am reminded of the flexibility that our ancestors used when introducing themselves in different areas. They would emphasise landmarks and histories to bring them closer to the locals. We do this now too. For example, when those of us from the Far North are in the Waikato we emphasise whatever genealogical links we can with our hosts. We use our *pepeha* (tribal mottos) and *whakapapa* (genealogy) to do this, linking the places and people of a bygone era to ourselves. One famous example is that one of the northern chiefs, Ueoneone, married two sisters, Reitū and Reipae, who were from the Waikato. By including recognition of this union, much celebrated in songs and chants, we reinforce those bonds, both ancient and modern. It is a kind of genealogical retracing of steps. A way to bring us together by recognising both our differences and similarities at the same time.

I can't help wondering how we could use *pepeha* as an approach to identify ourselves as global citizens. To emphasise connections with each other. This could be a platform for the dreams we need to manifest in the face of our climate emergency.

*Nō Papatūānuku ahau*, I am a descendant of mother earth. By identifying ourselves in this way we can firmly voice our global identity. It might seem like stating the obvious but in these dark times clarity of purpose is essential. We have nowhere else to go. It clearly locates us in that determination to uphold and protect our mother. A dedication to her, if you will. Firmly standing as global citizens using the ancient device, bringing the technology of *pepeha* forward, is one way to establish the manifesto of our aspirations for a healthier relationship with mother earth.

How could you add your connection with our planet as a whole to your *pepeha*? How could you build on that to incorporate your own personal link to our planet with your dreams for a better life?

# 21

# Kotahi karihi nāna ko te wao tapu nui a Tāne.

## The creation of the forests of Tāne comes from one kernel.

**Starting small leads to growth.**

Te Wharehuia Milroy

This *whakatauākī* reminds me of the importance of keeping going and being true to what I believe in. This is the path to a meaningful and solid place to stand for generations to come. All those small steps, the planting of tiny seeds, the ideas, providing role-modelling that our *tamariki* and *mokopuna*, our children and grandchildren, soak up. Just like seeds, they are germinating.

I made a terrible mistake. I thought it was better to have my children choose to learn *te reo Māori* (Māori language) when they were older. I was completely wrong. I don't know where I got the idea from as there is so much evidence that learning languages is easier when we are younger and so good for the brain. I should have planted that seed sooner rather than later.

My children have made up for my mistake, fortunately. My son, a teacher, learned some *te reo* during his teacher training when he was required to deliver his *pepeha* (traditional greeting), conduct a *mihi* (welcome) and lead a *kōrero* (discussion). He asked if he could come with me to visit our *rohe* (tribal area) in order to prepare and learn. My daughter, out of the blue, decided she also wanted to learn our language, to learn her *pepeha*. The seeds were waiting for the right moment to sprout without me realising it!

So the big lesson for me was to prepare the right kind of conditions, plant seeds and then be patient. Wait.

Just like the lush forest of Tāne (the deity of the forest), which keeps regenerating after being cut down to make way for farms in the past, so our language, indigenous to our country, grows back in unexpected ways.

The world does seem pretty bleak right now. This *whakatauākī* reminds us that small steps, planting those little seeds, all those actions, they add up. And together, as a collective, these tiny seeds of hope multiply and germinate more and more *aroha*, courage and kindness. An *aroha* forest, if you will. With deep interwoven root systems and airy canopies for the flourishing of healing wisdom and courage for generations to come. Let's follow Tāne's lead in matching the sacred forest with our own emotionally rich forest of connectivity and *aroha*. Planting our small seeds of action and progress now and build a strong, interlacing future for generations to come. A forest of *aroha*, courage and kindness akin to that of Tāne.

# 22

# Me te toroa e tau ana i runga i te au.

Like the albatross nestled upon the current.

**Manifesting resilience with the elegance of nature.**

I saw albatross in Antarctica in late 2019, on a Homeward Bound voyage to the coldest, driest place on earth. They glide through the air with unspeakable ease. The albatross has a wingspan of more than three metres. Just measure that in your lounge, sitting room, garden. It is huge. Paying attention to birds was a key aspect of our ancestors' lives. They derived life lessons from birds, and this proverb is a serious compliment.

This *whakataukī* paints a vivid picture of the magnificent albatross sitting seemingly steadfast and robust upon the ocean currents. By convention this saying is usually applied to males. But for me the story is not confined to the good looks or fine clothes of a person, rather the additional ability to ride out the ups and downs of life. Such is the comparison the ancestors draw our attention to. I want us to get better at noticing and commenting on our boys' and men's attributes. And let's not stop there. Can we begin to own and value our own skills and attitudes of compassion and consideration?

I try to see others in this way. No matter how composed they may appear, every one's lives have slings and arrows. Everyone has pain and suffering. Even those of us who seem to have our act together have down days and struggle with unexpected events. For me this *whakataukī* speaks to our ability to tap into our truest nature. An albatross cannot be anything but an albatross. As humans we can lose our sense of identity in our desire to please others, in our work and home roles. We can lose that umbilical sense of self. Finding our place, our *tūrangawaewae*, literally our place to stand, can feel impossible when we become so lost.

Coming home to ourselves is always a possibility, is always an option, it may just appear hidden. Being in Antarctica with a group of 100 extraordinary women from science gave me the impetus to look at the examples around me with ancient eyes and listen to the learnings surrounding us in that potent environment. Nature is trying to give us messages all the time. We need to look up from our devices, lift our downcast gaze and rediscover our own beauty in living. Try it for yourself. Free yourself from distractions and focus on your inner stillness despite the surrounding hustle and bustle. Switch your device off even for one hour a day and see what a delicious difference it makes to your emotional wingspan.

# 23

# E kore au e ngaro, he kākano ahau i ruia mai i Rangiātea.

I can never be lost, I am a seed sown from Rangiātea.

**I have a reason for being.**

This is a well-loved *whakataukī*. It speaks to the heart of belonging. Rangiātea is a name of a port of departure of many ancestral *waka* (ocean-going canoes) in our ancient homeland. Naming this ancient place brings us home to a huge sense of comfort and reassurance.

We are all seeds blown on the ancient winds from our ancestors. Our old people knew that there would be times when we would feel completely lost. Bereft, hopeless and helpless. And they knew we would need resources to believe that things could change, that we could activate this energy from time immemorial in order to slowly but surely find our way back to our true selves.

The word for the winds, *hau*, is very powerful and used in many contexts. *Ngā hau e whā*, for example, literally means the four winds and refers to people from all corners of the earth. The winds continue to play a significant role for us, as you could imagine for a people who needed to know them intimately as ocean-going navigators. This *whakataukī* reminds us that these ancestral winds carry us forward. They never drop us, they never let us go. We are scooped up by these invisible caring hands. Seeds travel far and wide on the winds and eventually land and can lie dormant for long periods. When the time is right, when we are ready, we germinate. Little seeds of this ancestral home that can flourish in new places. I love the way this short proverb captures so poetically the potential already within us to be a modern-day conduit for ancient wisdom.

To me it highlights the presence of inner truths that can feel buffeted by the winds and which eventually settle, grow and become visible, no matter where in the world we end up. Because sometimes the winds of life can whisk us away to unexpected, far-flung places where it is hard to be true to our identity, our language and our customs.

We all carry the potential for growth passed down from earlier generations. This week, if you are feeling that wind sweeping you up and flinging you far and wide, hold onto this *whakataukī* and trust the *aroha* of your ancestors deep inside you to realise your potential when you come to your new place of rest.

# 24

# Tini whetū ki te rangi, he iti te pōkēao ka ngaro.

## A small cloud overhead will obscure the stars.

**A small group can overcome the multitude, can overcome a myriad of difficulties.**

Crystal clear, pristine white. Still water as far as the eye can see. My eyes try to take it all in. I feel them stretching to try to see the whole extraordinary vista. Te Tiri o te Moana, Antarctica.

Nothing could have prepared me for this starkly spellbinding place. My thoughts hark back to our

Polynesian ancestors Hui-te-Rangiora and Te Aru-tanga-nuku, estimated to have been in the Southern Ocean in the seventh century. What bravery and tenacity they must have had to pursue their dreams, no doubt following signs from *te taiao*, the natural world – birds, migrating whales, wind, currents, clouds. And here we are following in their wake, a group also following signs from nature, the acidification of the ocean, the catastrophic loss of bird and marine life, the changes in temperatures, storms, fires and floods. Forming our own small cloud of gritty determination to overcome the multitude of difficulties inherent to climate emergency. What would these courageous navigators make of the horrifying mess we have made of our precious planet? What are their messages hidden in this place?

I find myself advocating for the inclusion of indigenous knowledge alongside what is conventionally thought of as science. I feel a strong sense of responsibility. My stand, my role, as it turns out, is to reinforce the vital importance of Māori and other indigenous knowledge systems and processes of enquiry in providing critical evidence of how to protect and heal our world. It is unscientific to dismiss our body of knowledge.

Bringing forward our indigenous knowledge cannot be separated from *aroha*. This heart, this unashamedly emotional, caring knowledge is the missing element for action. This knowledge comes with such vibrancy and wisdom from ancient times, it is a wisdom about life, so fundamentally fused into our planet. We are the planet and the planet is us.

Our ancestors call to us as we gently pass the floating ice sculptures. They tell us to gather together and trust in our common goal of survival, of restoring biodiversity, and in this way we will overcome the problems our world faces. They remind us what we already feel, it is our stories, the meanings and the trust that telling those stories begins to build that will inspire us to do whatever it takes to restore our brilliant blue globe for future generations.

How can we build more trust in our families and neighbourhoods? What can we do this week to get together with our loved ones and share time that contributes to a greater sense of trust and shared truth? What stories can we share that bring us closer together and strengthen our resolve to restore the wellbeing we share with our planet?

# 25

## Te manu kai miro, nōna te ngahere; te manu kai mātauranga, nōna te ao.

The bird that eats the miro berries, theirs is the forest; the bird that consumes knowledge, the world is theirs.

**Application of your own knowledge opens up your world.**

I have always loved this classic *whakataukī*. These wise words remind us of the resources all around us. And remind us that it is critical to be deliberate about how we use knowledge as a key to opening our eyes, as a key to opening our world.

The first thing about this proverb that affects me is that the berry represents what is obvious and is recognised as a food source. Knowledge, on the other hand, is not necessarily recognised as nourishment. So this speaks to the creative process, it emphasises the importance of seeing beyond the self-evident and seeking nourishment from more than the mere physical. And there is another part. Knowledge is not always that palatable. We learn about discrimination, about injustice, about pain and suffering. It is not fair. Life is not fair.

Our *tūpuna*, our ancestors, knew this. They bring us back to reality. Learning and the acquisition of knowledge is hard, it sometimes hurts, it has responsibilities that we must carry.

What kinds of knowledge could you apply to open up your world this week? In your relationships, in your work? What are the straightforward, undeniable berries staring you in the face?

What is the knowledge you need to apply to find out what might be beyond those berries? Take your time to ponder this. Then really chew that knowledge slowly and deliberately. What did you learn?

# Whanaungatanga

**Te aroha ki
ngā hononga**

**We are** born to connect. Born social. Strengthening our bonds with others is a central part of our lives. And when these connections are tested or feel broken, we struggle to know what to do. We can feel lost and distant. We can struggle to experience positive emotions. We sometimes use unhealthy ways to try to feel connected. We can spin out of control. Lack of connection has serious consequences. It is a sad irony in this age of social media that many people feel more alone and empty than ever before. Actively working to draw on the *aroha* that exists in the beauty of simple connections between people is the message of these *whakataukī*. Our ancestors' wisdom reminds us of ways to experience real connectivity in the *aroha* intimately woven between us.

# 26

## Ki te kotahi te kākaho, ka whati; ki te kāpuia, e kore e whati.

If a reed stands alone, it can be broken; if it is in a group, it cannot.

**When we stand alone we are vulnerable, but together we are unbreakable.**

Kingi Tūkāroto Matutaera Pōtatau Te Wherowhero Tāwhiao

When we look to nature we see *kākaho* (reeds) growing together and they are almost impossible to break as a group. Try it. It's hard.

Our ancestors knew that, like these reeds, if we come together as a collective, with a sense of belonging, with a shared purpose, we are at our strongest too.

I interpret this message to mean that not just when we physically come together, but emotionally and spiritually unite, share how we feel, seek support from and be supportive of each other, we strengthen our personal and collective wellbeing for the good of everyone.

This *whakataukī* takes me to a sad and powerful lesson in my life. My younger brother killed himself. His experience of mental illness made him feel more and more alone. He felt different. He told me once that he didn't want to infect the rest of us with his sense of difference. He set himself further and further apart. Eventually, he made that horrifying decision to be at a fatal distance from us all and took his own life.

Our experience as a *whānau* (extended family) has been so deeply painful I didn't speak about it for many years. For one thing, I couldn't find words.

How to describe such loss and pain? This experience is one reason I became a psychiatrist – so I could work alongside those living with suicidal thoughts, and support them to stay alive, and support their families. I want to rid the world of suicide. Some might say that is ridiculously impossible. Well, I am all for attempting the seemingly impossible.

In our world, instant gratification, through buying things and social media, for example, is used as a quick route to happiness. But the real cost to ourselves and others is too high. If we are not careful, we will lose our connection with others, lose real intimacy and human bonds, instead becoming more isolated and alone.

And for men, like my brother, the isolation and expectation of our society can tip them into a terrifyingly desperate state. If we are going to find solutions that work, we have to get to the source.

What effect does our parenting have on the conventional male and female roles?

How do we have compassionate relationships across genders in our society?

How do we redefine collective human experience that transcends genders?

How do we stop playing out toxic, corrosive gender roles?

Most critically, how do we show our younger generations, by doing and not just talking, so they see and feel freer of gender restraints and more able to talk and support each other?

Separation, isolation and loneliness are destructive and, at their worst, they are killers.

Collectiveness, togetherness and closeness, as our Māori ancestors knew, are what make us strong and less breakable. When I look at clumps of reeds I notice they move gently, sometimes closer, sometimes a little further apart. This helps me to think about the practicalities of being close but not feeling smothered or overwhelmed. I let my *whānau* know I am there, by calling, texting, by just hanging out in our PJs. And there is space too. Healthy space in our relationships. I am also all for letting the *whānau* know this is a work in progress and I might get the proximity and distance a bit wrong sometimes but, like the reeds, we let it flow.

# 27

**Ko te hoa tino pono rawa, ko tērā e toro atu ai tōna ringa ki tōu, engari ka titi kaha ki tōu manawa te kōhengihengi.**

A true friend is someone who reaches for your hand but touches your heart.

***Aroha* goes straight to your heart.**

Te Wharehuia Milroy

Really good friends are so incredibly precious and this *whakataukī* reminds us of that. I feel so lucky to have friends I have known and who have known me for many, many years.

I love the simple beauty of the idea that the touch of hands can, on rare moments, also touch the heart. The reciprocity between and amongst friends is so important and the delicate balance of what true friendship means is hard to pinpoint, a balance between acceptance and honesty, the timing of when to broach the tough stuff and when to be a supportive champion. I remember one of my oldest friends telling me after I had a health scare that I looked 'bloated'. I was shocked and a bit hurt initially. But she was right. I had not been looking after myself. This was the catalyst for taking care of myself again. I am so grateful to her for being brave and taking a risk by sharing that with me because it touched my heart.

Friendship, like any relationship, is not all moonlight and roses. I have been witness to some terrible upsets between mutual friends and it hurts everyone involved, because when the heart is involved, feelings can be fierce.

We want to protect our friends, we want to share life's lessons. But sometimes as friends we have to be there simply to bear witness to sorrow and pain. We cannot fix things. And we sometimes get it wrong – we misread the role we are meant to play in that moment.

But there is a special glue between us and our closest friends. I cannot imagine my life without my friends. I am so grateful to them. They have got me through some very tough times – mostly by breathing the same air and making cups of tea! I am not a psychiatrist with my friends or myself, I am just me, warts and all. And that is enough, because we are friends. We touch each other's hearts.

Friendships can change too. The classic shift can come when friends get into new romantic relationships and have less time for each other. Sometimes friends can become judgmental and stuck in a negative mindset. I approach these situations from the perspective of everyone doing the best they can. And there are times to recognise that it is time for that friendship connection to change.

How have friends touched your hand and heart? How do you let your friends know about the *aroha* you feel for them? Let these precious friends know what they mean to you this week.

# 28

# He tao rākau e taea te karo, he tao kī e kore e taea.

A physical strike can be warded off, a tongue lashing cannot.

**'Sticks and stones may break my bones but words will never hurt me' is a lie.**

Mau rākau, our traditional Māori martial arts practice maintains the mental and physical dexterity of a bygone era. There has been a resurgence of these practices all round Aotearoa, New Zealand, with people ascending the grades of proficiency within this ancient art form. The ability to parry a blow from your opponent's *taiaha* (wooden weapon) is one living example of this well-known *whakataukī*. On the other side, we see the eloquence of speech-making, *whaikōrero*, on the *marae* (traditional meeting places). It is another form of language – formal, poetic, where the drama of oratory skills is used to great effect. It is in this setting that pointed, even barbed, commentary can be used publically where those attacked cannot retaliate so easily. These rebukes cannot always be directly responded to in the same way the thrust of a rākau (weapon) can.

I have always felt deeply uncomfortable with the idea that words can't hurt. Our bruised hearts cry with the wounding that comes from words. And these hurtful words can resonate over years.

I remember being told I was a 'TV bimbo' when I was training in psychiatry, having already completed my medical training. I was blindsided. What a cheap way to put me down. Nevertheless it stuck in my head and created doubts.

Now I look back and wonder why I wasted energy worrying about those words. But words matter and, at different times in our lives, we are perhaps more susceptible to their power.

Those words aimed to put me in a box. Those words were designed to constrain and define me; preclude me from being anything else. And what is a TV bimbo anyway? All the women I know who work in television are skilled and dedicated people.

Why do we humans try to label each other?

I see it in my work with people who have challenges with their mental health and unhealthy relationships with substances, people who are subjected to violence in relationships. The general response is often centred around describing some flaw in the person themselves. They should 'harden up', they are 'weak', they should 'just stop', 'just leave'. When people recover on their own terms and journey past being defined by their experiences of mental distress, addiction, violence, somehow society struggles with this shift. And this is so strange because there is another narrative we hear about speaking out and not being afraid to share pain and getting help when you are under stress or not coping.

This *whakataukī* reminds us that the words we speak, and the words we think, are powerful. The words we use to describe ourselves and others and our world shape the relationships we have and the way we feel. What words do you find escaping your lips that you notice labelling yourself and others?

Maybe there are words you use in your internal conversations that put yourself down, or criticise yourself harshly. This week, pay particular attention to your words of self-judgment. How could you have found alternative words that highlight positive qualities and potential?

# 29

Ko te maumahara kore ki ngā whakapapa o ōu mātua tīpuna, e rite ana ki te pūkaki awa kāore ōna hikuawa, ki te rākau rānei kāore ōna pakiaka.

# To forget one's ancestors is to be a brook without a source, a tree without its roots.

**Know where you come from.**

Te Wharehuia Milroy

Our ancestors are with us every day. Whether we like it or not. Whether we acknowledge their presence or not. Many of us have photographs of them in our homes. We see them in carvings and *kōwhaiwhai* (decorative ornamentation) in our meeting houses. We talk and sing about them. Their exploits, their adventures, their mischief, their determination in the face of hardship. We are their representatives on earth right now.

How did we lose touch with the wisdom of our ancestors? Where did we learn to discount and discredit it, to marginalise it? To step over those ancient, well-worn paths of knowledge about human harmony and discord, about our planet, and all of the intricate ecosystems within our world?

How did we risk becoming trees without roots? And why?

Remembering those who have gone before unlocks some solutions to the challenges of raising our babies today. In my work, I remind families about the power of our ancestors and the lessons they have to share if only we would look back and gather those care-giving insights to help us live into the future.

Many of our families do not fully understand the importance of babies' emotional needs. The modern world has stripped away many of the basic skills of nurturing babies in this way. So much financial pressure on families to work to pay the bills means that time with our babies is in short supply. Our societies do not prioritise the emotional needs of children.

We know that for ideal development, babies need many adults nurturing them, spending time with them. But the way our society works has turned this on its head. We have childcare organised so that many babies are nurtured by a few grown-ups. Child development experts and our ancestral wisdom are in agreement, the way indigenous societies focussed on loving babies was optimal. One way I try to empower *whānau*, families, to reclaim and regain skills of loving babies is to remind them that these babies are ancestors too.

One day people will look at photos of these babies as they grow up. Their descendants will sing songs and tell stories of their adventures. When I talk about these babies as ancestors I see a new light in the eyes of the family and the caregivers. Where the adults were feeling at a loss, inadequate and disheartened, I see those tiny sparks of hope turn to flame. I see the family begin to see their responsibilities in a new way. I see them rise to the challenge of bringing up these baby ancestors of the future. I see such energy for reclaiming and reconnecting with that line of ancestral wisdom and love that reaches back to time immemorial and now begins to stretch forward into the future.

We are all ancestors. We all have access to that unique ancestral call which can start within our own families. Then that influence radiates out into how we see our world, with ancestors' eyes and ancestors' actions. How can you bring forward your role as an ancestor this week? How do you want people to talk about you when you are no longer alive? How can you shift into that positive legacy mindset this week?

# 30

## He au kei uta e taea te karo, he au kei te moana e kore e taea.

You may dodge smoke on land, but you cannot dodge the current at sea.

**Learn to spot signs of danger.**

Smoke is such an ephemeral and yet devastating element. Smoke was used by our forebears as a signal of danger, from one vantage point to the next. In the open air, smoke can signal danger across long distances so that we can take precaution. It can also overwhelm and kill.

Currents of water are as dangerous; they are harder to see and harder to avoid. As ocean-going navigators of the largest expanse of water on the planet, our old people knew the ocean like the back of their proverbial hands. Ever been dumped by a wave? You have felt some of the sheer terrifying power of the ocean. Tangaroa and Hinemoana, our deities of the ocean demand respect. The old people used these daily influences on their lives, with the play on the word '*au*' meaning both smoke and current, to make us think about these as metaphors for signals of human behaviour.

For me, this *whakataukī* is about the dangers of relationships. Some signs of danger are obvious, like smoke, and some are hidden, like the currents. Smoke is easy to spot, it can be seen and smelt. Sometimes it leaves soot on your clothes and skin. Similarly, a human connection that is not healthy can leave a very clear mark.

Currents in open water are more complex and disorientating – the tides, the depth, submerged rocks, sea creatures, the winds, reflections of the sky and clouds. It is harder to pick up on currents and, before you know it, you can be, literally, carried away.

I have become an avid *waka ama* paddler and so I'm now out on the ocean regularly. *Waka ama* is our Māori name for an outrigger canoe, the *waka* being the main boat and the *ama*, the arm attached to the side by two struts to provide stability. I am lucky in that I live on an island and we can paddle off either the northern or southern coasts, depending on the winds and weather. So now I have become much more aware of currents in the ocean than I was before I got involved with *waka ama*. It fascinates me that unless we have to, unless we are forced to, we have so little knowledge of what could be considered the basics of the ocean. And the basics of human connections too.

We often lack the navigational tools to notice the emotional currents that can have such influence on our lives, and not always for the best. I know that for me, I can be strongly attracted to a certain type of romantic partner that in reality is not good for me. But I don't spot the pattern while I am being taken by the current! I have had to face this reality, this pattern. That is the first vital step. I have learned to really tune in to myself and if something doesn't feel right, I pay attention to it. I have to be honest, it takes me a while. I was in the habit of not paying attention to these niggles, these tiny ripples, but I have got better with practice.

What currents might we explore in our lives? How can we make them more visible?

How can we make better decisions about how to navigate these intimate whirlpools in our lives?

Putting on my psychiatrist hat and reflecting on what my patients have taught me over many years, it often takes a crisis for each of us to recognise we have some blind spots in noticing those smoke signals and currents in the emotional seas we are trying to navigate.

Clearly, it would be better to try and prevent such crises. So I invite you to take an emotional inventory of your past relationships and try to be brutally honest. Sometimes we all need a bit of distance to see those patterns for what they really are. I can't advocate enough for time spent alone. Taking time and space to process the end of one relationship before embarking on another. Not something I have always done and I now see how vital that is for my own wellbeing. I imagine myself looking out across the ocean from one of my ancestral mountains and being able to see the currents like ropes in the ocean and smoke signals on the horizon. We often hear about the importance of time. Let's remember to create plenty of space, plenty of distance in our lives to truly appreciate those emotional signals well before they are right up close and personal, and harder to see for what they really are.

# 31

# Ko te whaea te takere o te waka.

## Mothers are the hull of the waka.

**Mothers are integral to the waka of our lives.**

Our *whakapapa*, our genealogy, is filled with extraordinary Māori women leaders. From my own whakapapa, I have Waimirirangi, Turikātuku, Dame Whina Cooper, Dame Naida Glavish, Whaea Moe Milne to name just a few. Some people mistake our customs as placing women in a secondary role. This is not the case. Women as the '*whare tangata*', the house of people, the source of future generations, are revered in our culture. Practices where women sit behind men do not denigrate women. We are seen as extraordinarily precious, to be protected from harm. Our voices are the first voices heard on our *marae*, our traditional meeting places. Our *karanga*, our call, into the spiritual realm, between women from the home people and the visiting group, sets the scene for the discussions.

My mother, our *whaea*, died when I was pregnant with my son, nearly 30 years ago. I felt like I moved up a generation when she passed. It felt like I was stepping into her shoes and they were too big for me to fill. The loss has continued to be profound. When she died, I remember my daughter sidled up to me and quietly took my hand. She was three years old. I looked down and saw she was wearing a pair of my mum's heels. It made my heart smile.

My mother led me along an extraordinary path after her death. It feels like she left me clues to follow. She gifted her body to the medical school, something very uncommon in our culture as many of us believe in the sanctity of all parts of the body being buried together. But as a *whānau*, extended family, we agreed to support her dying wish. My father and I got to know the medical school and, strangely enough, the person we liaised with there was to become one of my teachers, later a PhD supervisor, and latterly my boss at Brain Research New Zealand. My mum showed the way.

At medical school I was the eldest female Māori student in my year group, so certain cultural practices were my responsibility. For example, the *karanga*. I remember vividly, on a student trip in Tūhoe, I felt my mother beside me as I called to the women of the *marae* there. When people ask me how I know I am Māori, I recount that story. My Māori identity comes from our women, from our mothers.

In my work I have seen many mothers with their families over the years, many families who have lost mothers, and many where there are long-standing rifts between mothers and their children. These are some of the most deeply painful situations to bear witness to. I am always looking for opportunities for healing and for the inclusion of mothers, especially when other *whānau* members are adamant their mothers are the problem.

When we explore deeper layers of a person's trauma, I often find that intergenerational trauma reveals itself and that the issue is rarely actually the mother. Mothers often cop the brunt of what we might best call 'projections', the negative ideas we have about ourselves that we see in others and what upsets us about them.

Our mother had only a few rules. One was she would never let us go to sleep on an argument. She would listen and cuddle my brother and me as she listened to us both. She had a great sense of humour and knew how to see the funny side of things. And she was a great cook. We always sat down for our family meals. These are the simple traditions I have tried to carry on.

My mum continues to have the most critical impact on my life. I have a chat with her most days. She remains my yardstick. She is still the *takere*, the hull, of my *waka*, canoe, and my journey is better for that.

How is your relationship with your mother? How can you realign your relationship, how you see her, and her life's journey, whatever the pain between you?

# 32

# Ehara taku toa i te toa takitahi, engari he toa takitini.

My success is not mine alone, it is the success of the collective.

**No one gets there alone.**

Survival was determined by the collective back in the day. Our ancestors knew full well that successful collective enterprise was the key to a good outcome. Hence this *whakataukī* lives on.

This is a very well-known saying which continues to have lessons for us in the way we manage our private and public lives and, most crucially, how we remember who we are as we navigate these two worlds. Let's face it – the divide between public and private is getting really blurred.

Many people share private things in the public arena in ways that they would not have had a mechanism for and that would not have been acceptable several years ago. For some this is even a major part of their job – influencers (youtubers, bloggers, instagrammers . . . ) make their living from sharing curated aspects of their private worlds in a public space. Managing the right amount of sharing is at the heart of success in social media – you want to avoid oversharing but, on the other hand, too little sharing can invite scepticism. Getting the balance right is not easy.

My role in Māori health means I am accountable to my community. I am held up as a role model. As a psychiatrist, I keep people's confidences. Without that trust I cannot do my job. I like to think I am a bystander to the world of social media, but I post things, I share things. Things are posted that include me. There are aspects on social media that are connected to me and over which I have little or no control.

For some, the blurring of boundaries between private and public can cause real problems. I had a stalker once who made such serious threats to me and my family that I had to get a harassment order. I share this to illustrate that some people struggle when the public versus private boundaries are unclear to them, as this stalker did.

I have also witnessed the positive outcome and sense of unity amongst young women in the context of disclosure of domestic violence in relationships. While there is some tolerance for real descriptions of pain and suffering, there is also major push back when people speak about family violence and the realities of controlling aggression from partners and family members. Getting voices of these experiences heard takes real grit, courage and perseverance to get through the push back. Look at what happened with #metoo. Initially there was a lot of scepticism and other women defending abhorrent male behaviour. As the momentum grew, with increasing evidence of real women telling their stories despite the ridicule, the tide turned. I still struggle with the fact that this only started in 2017. How did we get to this era and not sort this out?

All this adds up to more and more of everyday life being lived with public scrutiny. Your employers check your Facebook and Instagram profiles and posts, for example. So, when you feel those additional pressures of a 'public' life, you need extra support from trusted people in order to stay grounded and true to yourself and your own values. Otherwise there is the risk of spinning off out of control in response to trolls who attack the way we look, our opinions, and what we stand for.

How can we do this? For me, my cultural practices are key. When I introduce myself I sing, *waiata*. Where I am from women sing before we speak. It makes me feel good to continue this practice and it reminds me who I am. I also use the Māori language whenever I can, especially when introducing myself. This introduction is called the *pepeha* – it begins with your place in the world, the nature you live alongside, your ancestry and community and lastly introduces you. You can find my *pepeha* on page 3 introducing my ocean, mountain, river, ancestral canoe, meeting house, my tribes and then me right at the end. It is a fascinating process designed long ago to keep us humble.

The *pepeha* is just one reminder in Māori culture that we are one small part that comes right at the end of the story. The main protagonists are the lands and waterways, which have been here for millennia and which will live on beyond our meagre existence. Saying the words out loud is powerful for me, those words ground me in real places where I can reach out and touch my own history. I am just a tiny part of the continuum. Where are the places in your world where you can find that reality check touchstone? Where are the landmarks of your heritage, the songs of your childhood that contain the time capsule provided by your ancestors? That healing is available to us at any time.

# 33

# He toka tū moana, he ākinga nā ngā tai.

Steadfast as the rock that scorns the lashing tides.

**You are always there for me.**

My first thought is that the rock represents Māori wisdom and the ocean in *te ao hurihuri*, the ever-changing world. I picture the rocks in the ocean I see from my window on the ferry as I travel to and from Waiheke Island. How the water touches the surface of the rocks often with the lightest caress, other times with the full might of Tangaroa, one of our deities of the ocean. The relationship between rock and ocean has been ever-evolving. Where there is no rock, I cannot see the ocean in the same way.

The phrase *toka tū moana* also speaks to me of the familiar and contrasting experiences of life, that I can really relate to. Sometimes I feel like the ocean – turbulent, swirling, with tidal peaks and troughs. One minute I feel still and tranquil. Occasionally, life can feel like a raging tempest around me. And sometimes I feel like the rock.

As a psychiatrist I need to channel my inner rock, to be a predictable, reliable touchstone. I also need to have flexibility like the water, to ebb and go with the flow where my client, my patient, takes me.

Being a rock means having patience. Waiting, just being present, it's as simple as that.

I also think of *tikanga* (Māori cultural lore) as a rock in my life. I have been in challenging situations where having *kaumātua* (elders) present always proves a vital support. The power of *karakia* (prayer) and the power of *wairua* (deep spiritual connectivity) are so clear in my work. These are things that might feel alien to some of you. Back in the day our old people prayed for everything. Prayers for walking in certain areas, prayers to invite a successful fishing trip, prayers for pregnancies, babies and for the dead and dying.

Nowadays we have a range of prayers – some Christian, some non-Christian, some from special Māori religious faiths. I always offer a prayer at the beginning and end of all my consultations and reviews, at team meetings. For me this is a way to settle the collective energies and set the scene for quality interactions and insights for more cohesion and better listening.

Perhaps there are new family traditions you could establish that include things that are said with solemnity, or prayers if you prefer. This is one way to settle ourselves and others into a collective sense of peace. A place where the rock and the ocean co-exist. Where turbulence and steadfastness can just be.

Maybe you are, at times, the rock and maybe, at times, the whirling ocean in need of the rock. Who has been your rock? Who has helped you to go with the flow?

# 34

# He manako te kōura i kore ai.

## Hope won't get you the crayfish.

**Don't count your chickens before they hatch.**

For me this *whakataukī* is about fully engaging in our own destiny. It is about following through on what we believe in. It is about the authenticity of our behaviours. This leads to discovering the real blessings we can experience in life.

And yes, anything to do with crayfish gets my attention. Such a delicious gift from Tangaroa, the ocean. We usually have crayfish for lunch on Christmas day. Such a treat!

To put this *whakataukī* into practice we must first believe in the existence of our 'crayfish'. We need to have at least some sense that the benefits of our endeavours exist rather than focussing on the negatives. We don't want to put our hands into the underwater cave to grab hold of a conger eel!

There is plenty of work to be done in advancing our chances of achieving our goals. Just like the crayfish diver, preparation is everything. And preparation is about learning. We need to know where we might find our goals and all the baby steps to get there. We have to put the work in, we need to have skin in the game as they say. Missing out steps along the way is not going to get us to the goals we set. Neither will behaviours that sabotage our goals. It takes guts and determination over a prolonged period and, even then, we may not achieve the goal we set out to reach.

In our *waka* tradition of traversing the oceans in canoes, navigators did not set goals of discovering islands as we understand goal-setting today. They observed the migratory birds without webbed feet and they knew there was land over the horizon. They knew that the islands were out there, in the great Moana-nui-a-Kiwa, the Pacific Ocean, they just had to go and fish them up.

My aim has been to lead my best life I could, through being the best mother, the best doctor I can be. I have told my kids from time to time, 'This is a work in progress.' I am going to make mistakes, I am trying my best. There is no manual. Hoping for the best with the kids is not too helpful. Hope is necessary but it is not an action. It doesn't equip any of us with ways of being together and learning from each other. It is an important platform, but hope alone doesn't do the trick of enabling real life transformation and happiness. Putting into practice all those baby steps in relationships, at work and with ourselves, is what counts towards tangible shifts towards a deep inner sense of wellbeing.

Not taking life for granted is the key take-home message. Appreciating all that life offers us is not always easy or straightforward. Remembering that the preparation and work that you have put in will come to fruition eventually, just like waiting for those chickens to hatch, you can't rush that part. How can you surrender this week and allow patience to be a part of your day? What if you have already done all that can be done and you only need to wait for things to fall into place?

# 35

## Moea te wahine o te pā harakeke.

Marry the woman of the flax cultivation.

**Be a woman who thinks about her legacy.**

I have often sat with this *whakataukī* and wondered about an interpretation that we as modern women can relate to. Seemingly this is an instruction to men back in the day to ensure they considered the nurturing skills of prospective partners vital for the group's preservation. But what relevance does this have today? We live in a world beyond binary ways of considering gender for one thing. Looking beyond the superficial layers is key. Our extraordinary *te reo Māori* (Māori language) teachers often say that our language is akin to that of William Shakespeare because it is both poetic and also gets right to the heart of the matter.

*Te pā harakeke* is a metaphor for the extended family and for generations to come. So it makes sense to me that this *whakataukī* is about someone whose focus is firmly in the legacy camp. We are those people. We think about the future. And what kind of a future we want to build for our younger generations, not only our own biological children, all children. The big issue staring us all in the face is the wellbeing of our planet.

Can you breathe underwater? No, neither can I. The climate emergency is confining some world citizens to live under water. Some of their lands are already submerged.

So for me this *whakataukī* is about being the people who speak up for this injustice. And there are lots of small things we can do to show we are committed to a better future. Meat Free Mondays is a programme we have established on Waiheke, the small island where I live, following the growing number of global initiatives promoting eating differently as a way to reduce carbon emissions from traditional dairy and meat farming practices. Making just one day meat-free is doable. It is achievable for many people. And it makes such a difference to our world, to our bodies and to our sense of spiritual connection to all living beings. The evidence is clear. By reducing our consumption of meat even just a little we can help to reduce these emissions, which is great for the planet, we help our bodies to be healthier and we deliberately choose to think about what we put inside our bodies. It gives us a sense of contributing to a better world so easily.

What is your legacy? What would you like people to say about you at your funeral? What are some small steps you could take to bring legacy into your daily life right now? Legacy is all about progress, not perfection. How will you nurture your *pā harakeke* today?

# 36

# Ahakoa whati te manga, e takoto ana anō te kōhiwi.

Although the branch is broken off, the trunk remains.

**Misfortunes will not undermine an individual or group if the foundations are strong.**

Crying. It is something we try to hide sometimes. I know I do. I have cried in the stairwell at the children's hospital where I work, more than a few times. Horrible things happen to people and it hurts. Sometimes it cuts so deeply, it feels unbearable.

Our forebears often used trees and the sacred forest of Tāne, our ancient native canopy, as metaphors to talk about the loss of people from our extended families, tribes and communities. To express this loss and to give hope and strength to those trying to cope.

This *whakataukī* fills me with a sense of purpose for my *whanau* (extended family) for my patients and communities, despite my hurt. We lose our loved ones. It is heart-breaking. My Aunty Rata passed away recently and it hit me hard. She had been married to my mum's older brother and had been close to my mum. It was like losing mum all over again. It rocked me to the core. I remember crying on the way home. In fact, I had to pull over and stop the car. And then I remembered this proverb and it reminded me of all the people who came together to honour her and to celebrate what she meant to us, to share our memories of her, to keep her alive in our hearts. We are the trunk of that tree. We find ways to carry on and, even when we feel a bit wobbly, we reach out for each other, we come back to our memories, like layers in the trunk of a tree.

The *whakataukī* also reminds me of one of my favourite greetings.

*E ngā pūioio rau o te tōtara haemata o tō tātou nehenehe nui*. The multiple knots of the vigorous tōtara of the ancient forest.

Not a *whakataukī*, but an eloquent way to acknowledge a group of people who represent those areas where the branch has broken off and left a characteristic knot in the wood. These knots are hard, they are tough and resilient. Just like us as we hold the pain of our loss and find ways to continue to live with the wisdom the loss brings.

I notice that crying for my aunty, I was crying for all those I have lost, and crying for myself, my own frailty. Somehow this crying helped me to let my *aroha* be seen. It seeped down my cheeks, drop by drop. Crying has a strange ability to purify – such is the magic of *aroha* when it manifests in tears. The *aroha* of tears seeks to be witnessed by others. I am learning to be seen when I cry and not to hide it. The shared witnessing of this *aroha* opened up some more space in my heart. Who do you cry for? How could you let others see your tears this week and let them give you that sharing of *aroha* that opens up more heart space?

# 37

## He hono tāngata e kore e motu; kā pā he taura waka, e motu.

Unlike a canoe rope, a human bond cannot be severed.

**Loving human connections cannot be broken.**

You know that feeling when you just click with someone? When someone really gets you? Something about the eye contact. Something about the natural ease of interaction. It is the same feeling as a relaxing, long exhale of breath. This is precious. These are the signs that something very special is happening. Truly loving human bonds are being woven. It doesn't happen that often that we meet people in life with whom we are so easily open, loving and genuinely vulnerable. So when it begins to happen I have learned to savour these moments and to build on them.

Our ancestors' survival relied on these tight human relationships, both through bloodlines and friendship. Loyalty, honesty, shared goals for the future are all essential parts of our cultural goals passed down in this *whakataukī*. Our grammar gives us a major clue that friends are in a special category of connection. We use the 'o' form to describe the bond with friends, as we do to show our affinity and respect for those of our own and older generations in the blood ties within our *whānau* (extended family).

Our old people loved to use comparison and contrast to illustrate their point. The rope used to tie up a *waka* (canoe) would have been made of *muka*, a very strong woven fibre from *harakeke* (flax leaves). *Muka* is renowned for being incredibly strong. Parts of ocean-going waka were lashed together with *muka* ropes, so they had proven endurance. Even these hardy ropes could not compare to the powerful strength of close human connections.

What this *whakataukī* also tells us is that when human relationships are under stress, in conflict, seemingly in tatters, those fundamental links remain. It saddens me to say that I see many *whānau* where relationships within the family seem broken, on the surface. Whatever we can do to prevent the fraying of these bonds is imperative. And I have seen time and time again that, with support, these close human links can re-emerge stronger than ever, despite the storms of life.

Do you have some bonds with people you love that you could strengthen or rebuild this week? How can this *whakataukī* help you to begin that restoration?

# Tino rangatiratanga

Te aroha ki te tika

**Tino rangatiratanga,** absolute self-determination is about doing the right thing in the right way for ourselves and others. Standing in our own truth. But it is often a struggle to know what that truth is with so many competing and mixed messages all around us telling us who we 'should' be. How do we discover the ways to best take care of ourselves, to discover our true identities, in order to refuel our inner resources for the collective good? Our ancestors had great lessons for us in their *whakataukī*, which teach us to recognise our true selves. There is such *aroha* embedded in the practice of focussing on unearthing our genuine selves, on revealing our authenticity. These *whakataukī* enable us to use *aroha* as our navigational compass amidst the confusion around us. And with this *aroha*, we can grow into more fully formed representatives of those who have gone before.

# 38

## He kuaka mārangaranga, kotahi manu e tau ki te tāhuna, tau atu, tau atu, tau atu.

The flock of godwits have swooped up into the air, one lands on the sandbank and the others follow.

**Leaders and followers work together.**

Tūmatahina

One of my famous ancestors, Tūmatahina coined this *whakatauākī* many generations ago. It came to him as he was leading one of our tribes away from the threat of invaders. He instructed the group to walk in his footprints on the beach so that the enemy would think there was only one person walking that way. Luckily he had really big feet! Tūmatahina used this saying to illustrate that following his lead was important. He used the *kuaka*, the godwit, a familiar example from nature to show effective human leadership can work like the birds. When one bird comes down to alight on the sand bank, it is safe and timely for others to follow. The picture he painted captivated the people and they followed his lead to safety.

The *kuaka* is one of our tribal *kaitiaki* (guardians). The bird is sacred to us – so important that it is enshrined in our deed of settlement with the Crown. Our ancestors were exquisite observers of the mannerisms and culture of these incredible creatures. One of our *tohunga* (experts) told me that *kuaka* take a small stone from the beach at Pārengarenga (their home in Te Tai Tokerau, the Far North of Aotearoa, New Zealand). They keep the stone in their gullet and this provides them with a navigational tool to find their way back home from the other side of the world.

When they fly, the older birds mentor the younger ones. Every so often younger birds are swapped into the lead positions of the flock to learn.

For me this *whakatauākī* is very much about the importance of relationships in teams, groups and families and how essential it is that everyone within that communal gathering shares the same values and has mutual respect for each other. This is easy to say but, in fact, really hard in practice. We lead by example. Like the birds, it is the activity of flight that demonstrates the commitment to survival. At the same time we are mere flawed humans and so we can only aspire to the clarity of vision of the *kuaka*. We say to our kids, this is a work in progress, we are working to restore our language to safety, and more than that, to have *te reo Māori* (Māori language) embraced in all aspects of life. And it is not surprising that this commitment is hard for many people to stick to no matter what.

When we speak our *reo tuku iho*, the language of our ancestors, our values flow naturally. For me it is the language of my heart, of *aroha*, and it brings me back to my happy place. By living this language where *aroha*, with all its life force for survival, passion, and grit for future generations can be seen and heard, we are like the *kuaka*. The long migratory journey of the language carrying our identity forward for future generations to meet us on that sacred sandbank.

*Aroha* is a value at the core of my identity as Māori. *Aroha* is not the same as romantic love, although it can manifest as that. It has many facets. It is an unstoppable force, a fierce advocate, a never-ending wellspring of creative energy and care for others. It is about seeing the good in people and acknowledging that people are trying their best. It is selfless and it is about nurturing the self. This is *aroha*, not constrained by logic. It just is. An eternal, mysterious force that we all yearn for only to discover it was within us all along.

# 39

# Ngaua te pae hamuti.

## Chew on the shit stick.

**Rise to the challenge. Get stuck in.**

I remember when I first heard this *whakataukī* and the explanation around it. I was in the *wharenui* (meeting house) Te Matapihi o te Rangi (The Window in the Sky) in Tokoroa, at a total immersion Māori language retreat. Such an apt name for a place of intense learning. The meaning of this *whakataukī* goes back to when our ancestors defecated by sitting on a piece of wood that acted as a seat, positioned over a deep trench or cliff. The piece of wood itself got a bit grubby, so you can imagine the idea of chewing on it is not particularly appetising.

One of the challenges set for Māori scholars learning the most sacred aspects of ancient knowledge was to chew on this wooden seat stick. The idea being that it tested their fortitude.

I'm not suggesting we each go to our bathrooms and chew on the toilet seat! For me this *whakataukī* is a reminder to face challenges square on. When anything gets too tough, don't turn away. Follow that feeling of difficulty rather than turning away from it. Do what feels right, and stick with whatever you're dealing with – a rough patch in a relationship, a hard task at work or, on a bigger scale, calling out companies and governments that perpetuate human rights violations or harm the planet, facing up to our responsibility to look after mother earth. Life is hard, get on with it.

What might that look like? I have tried to imagine what putting that *pae hamuti* in my mouth would be like. It would involve a fair amount of gagging. But in reality, if we make a mess, we have to deal with the consequences.

And in our own lives, I think this *whakataukī* reminds us to also value each other and not pass on our pain to others, but to face our own trauma head on. Chew on that.

# 40

# E kore te pātiki e hoki ki tōna puehu.

## The flounder does not go back to the mud it has stirred.

**Sometimes you've just got to walk away and keep on walking.**

In some parts of New Zealand, pātiki (flounder) are abundant. They can be found lying hidden in shallow waters in the mudflats – perfect for spearing on the incoming tide. I am told if they get disturbed they only move a short way off, so you can catch them again once they settle into their new spot.

This *whakataukī* is a tough one because it reminds us we all have to own the mud that we stir up – the consequences of our actions. It may well be that we messed up some other people's mud too. When we stir the mud, it is vital to make amends, to say sorry, to communicate.

This *whakataukī* is also about recognising that the end is the end. Going back can just result in stirring up more mud and making things worse. I don't know about you but I have, on occasion, tried to go back – for example, to try again in relationships – and it just doesn't work.

It is an uneasy state of being when we are able to recognise there is nothing to be gained by returning to the stirred-up mud. Sometimes we prefer the mess we know to the vast unknown ahead.

I take courage from this *whakataukī* and the reminder to not look back. It is a salutary reminder that moving on from the disturbance that clouds the waters is good even when it is hard to see at the time. Are life's waters a little muddied at the moment? Are you contemplating rekindling your relationship with your ex? How might you use the lessons from this *whakataukī* this week?

# 41

# Kia mate ururoa, kei mate wheke.

Fight like a shark, don't give in like an octopus.

**Never give up.**

Tangaroa is one of the deities of the ocean. He and his offspring form all the creatures of the seas. For many of us whose peoples have been sustained by the ocean over generations, the sea is our *pātaka kai*, our food store. Our supermarket of time gone by, and for many it still is. This is why we are so vigilant in resisting activities that compromise the vitality of this resource and that connection with our ancestors and their practices. This *whakataukī* brings keen observations from the abundance of the ocean forward to highlight an important lesson about determination.

When a shark is caught on a fishing line it thrashes around furiously. Often the line breaks and it swims away. When an octopus is caught on a line it goes limp. Our ancestors were people of great principle, who believed in sticking to your values and fighting for what is right.

Nowadays, the world feels apathetic. Our political voting rates are low. People feel disengaged. There is a sense of powerlessness.

When I think of this *whakataukī* I see the fishing line and I see how exposed the shark and the octopus are. When we are exposed, what do we do – fight or go limp?

One stand-out example for me was being told I was 'outside the tent' at work – I was a contractor at the time for the health service. Apparently, I had no standing in the discussion around the direction of mental health services development, which would have huge impact on Māori because I was not a salaried member of staff. I was a bit stunned at this comment to start with. A bit octopus.

Then I got in touch with my inner shark.

There was nothing to see on the surface to show my transformation from octopus to shark, but I could feel that this comment had literally hooked into an issue I felt very strongly about and would fight for. I walked away thanking the person in my head for identifying this and reflecting that being excluded from that 'tent' was a good place to be, free of the constraints intrinsic to the self-appointed 'in' group.

We have many examples from history of people who have stood up for what is right, even when the chips were down. One of the most famous was when the words '*Ka whawhai tonu mātou, ake, ake ake!*', 'We will fight on for ever and ever!' were uttered at the battle of Ōrākau in 1864. Some say it was Rewi Maniapoto, others say it was a woman. Either way, this is the never-give-up attitude in action that gives so much oomph to us in modern-day battles.

When these 'hook' moments occur out of the blue, take a moment to consider if you want to fight. And then, never give up.

# 42

# Ngaro atu he tētēkura, whakaete mai he tētēkura.

When one chief disappears, another is ready to appear.

**No one is indispensable.**

There will always be someone better and more skilled that you. And that is okay. We need those that come after us to be better than us, to be better equipped for the rapidly accelerating future changes to and evolution of our world.

We are all important – this *whakataukī* isn't saying we don't matter. Rather, that we are all leaders, we are all chiefs in our own lives. We are in charge, even though it might not feel like it sometimes. The opportunity is always there to pick up the reins and decide to do it your way – to live the best version of your own life while being mindful of others. I am not suggesting that we live life with no thought to how others feel.

As the leaders of our own lives, we need to anticipate our own death. That might sound a bit heavy but we all know we will die at some point. When I talk to my kids about my *tangihanga* (traditional funeral ceremony) they recoil and say, 'Mum, that's so morbid.'

I disagree. And I know eventually they will get it. There has to be some succession planning around death. Making sure that we contribute to equipping those who come after is a critical part of our leadership role in our lives, and indeed on the planet.

It is interesting to ponder this in the context of climate change. Despite our best efforts to remain in denial, the next generations have shown astonishing leadership.

This *whakataukī* reminds me to take responsibility, to keep going, to keep sowing knowledge seeds so that, one day, someone from the next generation can step up, because that's what needs to be done.

# 43

# Nā te iho ko te kōrero, nā te whakaaro nui ko te mūmū.

## Talking comes naturally, silence comes from wisdom.

**Listening is underrated.**

Te Wharehuia Milroy

The people who listen and say very little are the ones to watch. This is something I have been taught by my *whānau*, my extended family. Silence is not an absence, is not a void. There is a lot going on in silence. On the *marae* (traditional meeting places) you can see the ones who listen intently, sometimes with their eyes closed. Don't be fooled. They are not asleep. They are so tuned in. Tuned in to the words, the tone of voice, the *wairua*, that is, the spiritual elements and vibrations that occur around the conversation. Talking is the easy part, this is the lesson.

Truly listening, hearing, being totally present is such an underrated part of human evolution. It can be a super power.

One of the things I invite parents I am working with to do is to think more deliberately about how they listen to their kids. Listening to their words is one thing but we also need to listen to what is behind the words – the feelings driving those words – and also to the silences.

How do we listen better? There are different kinds of silence and we need to notice all of them: hurt silence, lemon lips, the sad hush, the cold shoulder, the face like thunder, a withholding quiet.

There is a tendency for us to try to fill silence with a lot of words. This can sometimes be a way to avoid what we might feel in the stillness of quiet.

When we are not talking and we deliberately focus on listening, we have to stop, we have to be still.

When we stop, we can actually really notice how we feel in ourselves, what we are thinking. That can feel a bit scary.

For me, allowing for silence helps me really think about what I am saying – did I mean those words, was I just filling the void or trying to feel in control? Being still, listening to my own thoughts and taking some time to work out what is genuine is vital.

Listening to others, without interrupting them, without thinking about my response before they have even finished, is a useful discipline.

I have had to learn to slow down and stop, to truly listen to myself and others. I have learned the power of stopping and listening in silence.

See how it makes you feel.

# 44

# He aha te kai a te rangatira? He kōrero, he kōrero, he kōrero.

What is the food of leaders? It is communication.

**Good communication, internally and externally, is essential for leadership.**

My work as a psychiatrist is first and foremost about being with people as they discover that the answers and gifts they seek are already there. That their hearts are actually full of love and hope, even though pain and suffering is also present, and closer to the surface. Often it takes quite a bit of time for the person to feel that this pain has been truly acknowledged. Only after that time can self-love, care and nurturing begin.

I work with people at their most vulnerable and see them change how they view themselves, see how their self-knowledge develops – and how they communicate to themselves about themselves and others, and to the outside world. And from this, I get to witness the blossoming of self-leadership.

When I think about leadership I also think about who I feel compelled to follow. Who would I walk over broken glass for and why? There are some great leaders in the Māori world. The people I feel drawn to have put ego aside. They are genuinely, actively, visibly working with and for our communities. Their communication is giving. They talk openly about their vulnerabilities, about their mistakes. That is the kind of leadership communication I try to bring into my little corner of the world.

What have you noticed about the way you communicate and what you tend to feel most comfortable sharing? What would it take to talk about those awkward, scary parts of life where you felt more than a little out of your depth and yet managed to find a way through?

# 45

# Hōhonu kakī, pāpaku uaua.

## Deep throat, measly muscles.

**All talk, no action.**

Or as we say in my *whānau* (extended family), all talk, no trousers. I have no clue where we got that from, but it has stuck. Some people want the glory without the graft. And our ancestors knew it too.

We often use the word *ngākau* (heart) in front of an adjective to illustrate the type of person we are talking about. *Ngākau pāpaku* is someone who is shallow and frivolous. I have translated *pāpaku* as 'measly', you get the drift.

One very important role of *whakataukī* is that they warn us and remind us of traits and behaviours that do not serve the greater good.

Why don't people act on their words? Maybe they think it's not their job, maybe they feel they are too busy or overwhelmed with other things, maybe they don't feel confident, maybe they feel anxious, they may be blissfully unaware.

My approach is to say something like, 'I noticed you had some great ideas and then you weren't offering to participate in implementing them. What got in the way for you?' Or, 'How can we all get involved in making this happen? What part do you want to play?' I don't accept people avoiding contributing.

For me, the 'never leave anyone behind' rule wins in the end. How could you encourage some of your '*hōhonu kakī, pāpaku uaua*' friends and *whānau* to get involved this week?

# 46

# Ka pū te ruha, ka hao te rangatahi.

The old net is cast aside, while the new net goes fishing.

**A new sense of leadership.**

This *whakataukī* reminds us that our ways of doing things have a use-by date. The old approaches that are no longer useful are brushed aside as the new methods take over. Reflecting on the age of the smart phone and wearable tech, the accelerating pace of change, this can feel overwhelming. But we need face-to-face contact. Without it we erode our vital appreciation of the nuances of facial expression, body language and the beauty of the human voice. Without these subtleties, our ability to bring our best selves forward, informed by the richness of human connection, is eroded. We pay an enormous cost. We lose the delicate poetry of human contact.

This *whakataukī* has always intrigued me. The classical interpretation is about the next generation coming through, the next generation of leaders. I am interested in how we might consider the new net as the emergence of new chapters in our own lives, our own renewed sense of leadership and letting go of old ways of being.

My new net is about immersing myself in what I truly value. Moving away from a sole focus on what others expect of me. I think of the old net, which I know was not fully constructed by me. Sadly, some of the old net is a heavy, painful hand-me-down infused with suffering from generations before, added to by those who have wanted to control me and mould me into something that served their agenda. I want to craft my own net, reinvigorated with *taonga tuku iho*, the treasures of the ancestors. And with my purpose as their representative on the planet right now a central strand. The new net is made collaboratively with *whānau*, family and people I love. We can share the construction.

I am reminded of learning to make home-made pasta with a group of older Greek women. We chatted – I didn't understand most of what they were saying, but I know some of it was pretty juicy gossip. There was shrieking with laughter, there were dramatic pauses and eyes cast heavenward as tears of laughter rolled down our cheeks, as we gasped for each giggling breath. This is the kind of company I want to construct my new net. This new net will catch different fish depending where I choose to cast it. There will be no holes in my net. I am making it with *aroha*. I am now at an age and stage where I can truly accept myself, love myself and replenish the love I feel for myself and others as a source of energy for the power of good.

I can see my net, the more or less regular knots, the creative, less-regular patches, the spaces in between the *muka*, the strong woven threads of *harakeke*, flax. Can you get a sense of your new net – who will make it with you and what will you draw upon to bring it together? How could you imagine your new net coming together over the next week?

# 47

# E kore te kūmara e kī ake he māngaro ia.

The kūmara does not speak of its own sweetness.

**We do not boast.**

The *kūmara*, the sweet potato, is a prized vegetable. Many *marae* (traditional meeting places) have their own *kūmara* patches and storage areas. Our ancestors sailed from Polynesia to and from Latin America and this is how we came to have the *kūmara* as a prized vegetable, as a central part of our diet. On our local marae, Piritahi, on Waiheke Island, we have a long tradition of planting and storing *kūmara* because of its wonderful sweet flavour and ability to feed the multitudes with its goodness, passed down by our beloved Ngāpuhi *kaumātua* (elder), Kato Kauwhata.

The *kūmara* represents us. It acknowledges we are sweet inside, nutritious, we have much to give to the group. We feed each other. The *kūmara* grows from our gardens and gardening is a sacred activity – without it our people would have starved and died out. Taking care of the garden, of the *kūmara* patch requires skill. Rongo, our peaceful deity, protects our gardens and the work we do there. And how we communicate impacts profoundly on the collective. All of these layers are embedded in this short *whakataukī*. It sounds a critical warning – we do not boast.

This *whakataukī* has been hotly debated in recent years. Some have argued that we need to re-think the extremely humble sentiments. Our *tamariki* and *mokopuna* (children and grandchildren) need role models who can talk openly about our achievements, our journeys, our positive lessons in life. Others hold fast to the intention of ensuring we focus on the collective wins and resist the potential for bragging.

The powerful message in the debate about this *whakataukī* is that it illustrates how we can use these pieces of wisdom in a number of ways and for a number of contexts. For example, there is an emphasis not on the what, but on the how. It is the way we communicate our success that is crucial.

It is important for me that others assess my contribution by both the manner in which I act, as well as the content of what I do, not just what I say. It is the classic 'actions speak louder than words' scenario. Another important layer to this proverb is that words can be misinterpreted – what we say about what we do can be misread. Our actions and the ways in which these are completed are less likely to be misunderstood. This is because the manner in which we behave in the world reveals so much about our intentions and what we actually care about, compared to what we say. How do you follow through on your intentions, how do you put into practice what you believe?

What are the stories you tell about yourself? How do you describe your successes? How do you guard against arrogance and conceit?

# 48

# E toa ai a Whiro, me noho puku noa a Kou tāngata.

## All that evil needs to triumph is for good people to do nothing.

**Apathy breeds evil.**

Te Wharehuia Milroy

I often ponder what it is that creates and perpetuates apathy. One thing is for sure, our energy seems to begin to fizzle out in the face of the enormity of the problem of climate emergency. How can we as individuals or small neighbourhoods possibly make a difference to the climate emergency? We are good people, aren't we, trying to find ways that feel like they will have an impact, and getting disheartened at the sheer vastness of the climate emergency problem. Fires raging out of control. Floods, droughts, extraordinary storms happening with increasing frequency. It all feels overwhelming at times. You might be wondering, what can we really do on our own?

Saying no to single-use plastics, straws, plastic bags and wrappers now means that carrying such items is regarded as pretty shameful, and rightly so. Banding together in *whānau*, families and communities, to provide positive substitutes for plastics has been a great source of community activism and created new experiences of unity. But even now some people remain sceptical about these little changes and the shifting of norms. There is a shoulder shrug, and a shaking of the head. A defeatist sense of not having the wherewithal to make any kind of a difference.

How can we connect with those feelings and turn that learned helplessness into focus, determination and action? How can we reconnect with our purpose and our relationship with our planet and our oceans to propel us forward into a state where doing nothing is something we cannot tolerate. Children's questioning – 'What did you do?', 'Where were you?' – is one potent source of purpose. How can we possibly justify doing nothing when the planet is being so damaged? Seeing the increasing levels of anxiety about the future of life on earth in our young people fuels my resolve.

# 49

# E kitea ai ngā taonga o te moana, me mākū koe.

If you seek the treasures of the ocean, you'd better get wet.

**Life is for living.**

We screamed at the top of our lungs as we ran hand in hand into the icy waters. Running into the freezing waters of the Antarctic Peninsula is all at once a scary and life-changing experience.

The experience has made me view this *whakataukī* in a powerful new light. Yes, the proverb has always conjured up the reality of truly getting involved in order to discover ways to create positive change. Getting fully immersed in a purposeful and fruitful project has at its core the need for some sort of visceral experience. There is no way to avoid this. Staying theoretical, staying at a distance isn't going to cut it.

And there we were, immersed in this biting chill, getting wet and shivery in the pursuit of building connection with our mother earth. We felt our determination and our vulnerability at the same time. And these are the parts of ourselves where we need to provide leadership in this complex world.

Being immersed in those bright clear waters for just a few moments brought a rush of joy and at the same time intense shock to my whole body, mind and spirit. A massive cold jolt to the system. A reboot.

An unforgettable moment as they say. And yet the memory will fade. So how to hold onto the precious learnings of that moment?

What have been your moments of shocking realisation on the path to your own leadership in life? How do we capture those moments so that we can return to them? Refresh our experience of them to give us insight for the next chapter of our lives? Maybe this *whakataukī* can serve us in this way. *Me mākū koe!* Go get wet!

# 50

## E tū te huru mā, haramai e noho. E tū te huru pango, hanatu e haere.

Let the white hair remain here, let the black hair get up and go.

**We must follow our dreams.**

Nukutawhiti

Nukutawhiti was a famous voyager, born around 785AD, the grandson of the great Kupe. This *whakatauākī* is attributed to him.

When Kupe returned to the ancestral lands of
Hawaiki having discovered Aotearoa, New Zealand,
there was war raging. Nukutawhiti, his grandson,
asked to leave the war-torn home and go to Aotearoa.

The hair colour is the clue to this intergenerational
conversation which makes me smile. We parents
and grandparents, aunties and uncles are the
white-haired generation now. This is a lesson
for us to let go and support our younger ones to
pursue their dreams, away from the strife at home.

As older generations, we might like to think we are
urging the younger ones to explore, to travel, to
discover and understand the world and, in doing so,
to reach their potential. And yet we live in a world
of such fear and restriction about what younger
generations can do. There seems to be a shift of
focus which is more about young people conforming
to social norms – having economic stability, getting
into employment as quickly as possible are two
that are emphasised. Many families have not been
in a position to enjoy these aspects of life and so it
makes absolute sense to want those things for our
future generations.

What the *whakatauakī* is saying to me is let's make
sure that we do not restrict our younger generations

from following their dreams. Let's make sure they have access to all the choices they need, all the choices they wish for.

When I was growing up I was lucky enough to feel that the world was a more or less safe place. I travelled to China in 1985, spending two days on a train and then 5 weeks in Beijing when, at that time, it was a closed city. It was a magical experience that I will never forget. Cycling around Tiananmen Square with bicycles borrowed from the New Zealand Embassy in the middle of the night. Making dinner at home with the family of two Beijing opera performers. I was able to return to the NGO Conference on Women there in 1995. Witnessing the transformation of the city was awe-inspiring. I returned again in 2010 to speak at a conference and again I saw the incredible changes in the numbers of people, the developments alongside the retention of local traditions.

I have been truly blessed with opportunities to follow my dreams, experiencing other cultures, their languages and ways of life. This has brought home to me the importance of cultural traditions and language as the life blood of identity for people all over the world. I follow in the footsteps of Nukutawhiti. I have the travel bug passed down from many generations and I have passed it on to my kids. Something strangely fitting about travelling is coming home and having new appreciation for home and clarity about what is really important in living our best lives.

I wonder how we ensure opportunities to chase dreams continue to be available for generations to come? Indeed, how we make sure all our descendants have dreams they want to follow is critical. We lead by example. Encouraging, noticing, talking about our own dreams, and how we got up again when the dream didn't quite follow the path we wanted it to. The lessons we learned along the way. Have a think about what is possible for you this week in manifesting dreams in yourself and in those you love.

# 51

# Ruia taitea, kia tū ko taikākā.

## Strip away the sapwood, the heartwood remains.

**Shed those outer layers and reveal your internal courage.**

What is it going to take for us to live our best lives? Our most honest lives? I have now reached the same age as my mother was when she died and it saddens me to say that this has been my line-in-the-sand moment. I have no more energy for compromise. And I have to say, it's not that easy to let go of old patterns. With years of focussing on pleasing others and tuning in to what others need, it can feel impossible to know who we really are anymore, am I right? A deep sense of loss and grief floats up from the recognition that our true selves have become so blurry with all the covering and layers where they are hidden. And yet they are still there. Digging down through those layers, just like the outer layers of a tree towards the central core. The strong inner heartwood is right there.

Our ancestors used the metaphor of trees often. Trees of different types were studied for their various properties, for making different types of *waka* (canoes), homes, storage for food and for their medicinal properties. Their characteristics, their majestic height, their supple youth, their healing qualities, their shade and protection appear in metaphor.

Simply noticing trees is something I try to do every day. It might sound a bit odd at first but it reminds me that the internal heart and heartwood that we share with trees is always there even if there is a sense of it being obscured by the outer bark. Where I live there are some ancient *pōhutukawa* (coastal myrtle) trees that stand as guardians of the coast. They have magnificent clouds of ruby red blossom in the summer, the colour so vibrant and alive. Our ancestors are said to have believed these flowers were red-plumed birds when seen at a distance from their *waka* (canoe) on the ocean, red feathers being highly prized.

Do you have a favourite tree you like to sit in the shade of, or to watch from your window? How much pleasure do you feel watching the leaves change colour and fall at different times of the year, or seeing the branches covered in snow, or the wild rippling of leaves in the wind?

# 52

# Te rerenga o Hui-te-Rangiora.

## The journey of Hui-te-Rangiora.

**Follow in the footsteps of our ancestors, protect our planet.**

I wrote this *whakatauākī* as a cautionary reminder to hold fast to the memories of our ancestors. By telling their stories we reinvigorate our role as *kaitiaki* (guardians) of our beautiful mother earth.

Hui-te-Rangiora was a Polynesian navigator who journeyed to Antarctica in the seventh century. His route and those of others who have followed forged a path that we can follow. Our indigenous peoples from time immemorial have had a unique relationship with our world. One that is so strikingly intimate, paying attention to the genealogy of all members of the global family and living in a mutually respectful way with our earth.

Travelling along the Antarctic Peninsula, following in the footsteps of our great navigating forebears, is a very solemn meditation in recognising what is important.

Being in Antarctica strips away the trappings of life. She is a great equaliser. She shows us that what we call climate emergency is real. It might be better to call this an earth emergency. Antarctica, the cardiovascular system on our earth, the pump, the controller of currents and weather systems, she forces us to face what really matters. This is not some theoretical problem in a far-off universe. This is a home truth about our own environment. This is where we cannot fudge or pretend. Antarctica brings home these harsh truths about us and our disconnected, dysfunctional relationship with our planet.

Krill is not a creature I previously felt any affinity for. I cannot remember ever thinking so much about krill. I cannot recall thinking of krill as a relative! Having shared the ocean and seen the vital importance of krill in the food chain of life in our oceans, now I feel strangely close to our krill cousins.

Being in Antarctica, krill is something that cannot be ignored. Being there, the role of krill is right under your nose. Almost 80 per cent of the world's krill spawn in the Antarctic Peninsula. This just happens to be where the greatest populations of penguins, seals and whales live in the deep south, and krill is on the menu for all. Now the sea ice is receding there is less habitat for krill to shelter and feed.

So, you get the picture. No krill means no penguins, no seals, no whales. Can you imagine a world without whales? I don't want to imagine that, but now I am forced to.

And I am not alone. As a child and adolescent psychiatrist, I see children and families wracked with anxiety about the death of all whales, about penguins dying out, about seals becoming extinct.

Who is going to care about krill? Krill is not a member of our global *whānau* (extended family) that immediately captures our imagination. They are tiny and hard to see for one thing. Plus their story has been one of massive abundance. So how could we run out of krill, right? It turns out we can.

There are weird contradictions in this land of krill. On one hand, the insignificant nature of humans is writ large. The scale of the mountains and glaciers, the massive icebergs, the vast expanse of ocean. The sky that stretches your eyes. We are forced to face our puny inadequacy. Then we see the local creatures so in tune with nature. They fit in here, we don't. We are like aliens from outer space, not naturally equipped to survive. Without boots, thermals and our fleecy jackets, we would die here. But we also see our destructive human impact. What takes your breath away is to see the increasing damaging global effects on this local superficially pristine environment. The impacts on krill.

When will we stop and listen to the story Antarctica is trying to tell us? This is one story about our global family. Us, krill and everything else. As I say '*E noho rā*', 'farewell' to the land of krill, the lessons will stay in my heart, in my blood, forever. So saying goodbye to Antarctica hurts. Saying goodbye to family is always hard, especially leaving the little ones. I can't help wondering if krill had the same rights as people, hell, if the planet had the same rights as a person, what would we do? How would this shift our thinking, our behaviour and how we feel?

We are the planet and the planet is us. What is it going to take for us to take action to protect our planet? What steps can you take this week to make your difference, to play your part?

# Kupu whakatepe

Coming to the end of this book's journey.

**Finally, I want to leave you with a challenge — to write your own *whakatauākī*, a proverb with *aroha* for yourself.**

A: Allow yourself time to stop and take notice, for your own pleasure and growth.

R: Reflect on your favourite elements of nature and their connections to each other and to you and your life. Landscapes, birds, waterways, animals, plants. Think about your cultures of origin. What clues about the natural world and cultural meanings might be helpful to you? What characteristics of these parts of nature and our planet do you relate most to?

O: Organise some words and phrases about your favourite and most powerful and vivid images, memories about the natural world. What is the natural world trying to tell you?

H: Habits. Think about how your *whakatauākī* taps into your habits, things you notice about the ways you tend to do things at the moment or have done in the past. Be kind to yourself and if you are not being kind, notice this and wonder what that might be about.

A: Apply. What can you take from your own *whakatauākī* for right now? How might you apply it over the next week? Relax and enjoy your first *whakatauākī*. You might feel like writing a few more.

**Whakatauākī with *aroha*. A practice for deeper connection between you, your loved ones and our mother earth.**

# Index

acceptance 42–3
action(s)
  consequences of our 179–80
  failure to take 195–6
  mindless 33–4
  taking 83, 85–7
adrenaline rushes 34
adversity 93–6
age 90–1
Ahipara 77
albatrosses 101–2
All Blacks 86
ancestors 10, 23–4, 29, 42–3,
  47, 60, 74–9, 82, 90–1,
  94–5, 102, 106–7, 110–11,
  114, 120, 122, 129, 131–4,
  172, 174–5, 177, 182, 198,
  211–12, 216–17, 219–22
Antarctica 101, 103, 109–10,
  209, 219–22
anxiety 7, 17, 207, 221
Aotearoa (New Zealand) 4, 10,
  23–4, 76–7, 179, 212
apathy 182, 205–7
appendicitis 20
Atutahi (Canopus) 35–9
authenticity 155

babies 133–4
beauty 89–91
behavioural patterns, negative
  33–4
Beijing 213
being 105–7
birds 41–3, 73–4, 101–2, 173–6
boasting 201–3
bonds 167–9
busy lifestyles 25

canoes, ocean-going *see waka*
carbon emissions 160–1
challenges, rising to 177–8

childcare 133
childhood memories,
  reconnection to 32, 77–8
China 213
choice-making 33–4
climate emergency 70, 81–3,
  94–5, 110, 160–1, 186,
  205–7, 220, 222
collectives, strength of 119–22,
  145–9
communication 187–9, 191–3,
  197–8
community 9, 51, 64, 70, 72,
  82, 146, 148
conditioning 34
connection 5–6, 9, 63–4, 73,
  76, 79, 117–69
  avoidance 64
  erosion 198
  unbreakable nature 167–9
cooks 53–6
Cooper, Dame Whina 91, 141
courage 99, 147, 215–17

danger, spotting the signs of
  135–9
death 186, 215
deities 87, 89, 136, 181, 202
destiny 155
difficulties, overcoming
  109–11
dispensability 185–6
diversity 41–3, 93–6
domestic violence 147
'don't count your chickens
  before they hatch'
  155–7
dreams 93–6
  following your 211–14

emotions 16–17
endings 179–80

environmental issues 4–5, 10,
    67–115
    denial regarding 81–2
    taking action about 83
    *see also* climate emergency
evil 205–7
exhaustion 25
eyes 89–91

families, extended *see whānau*
fear
    banishment 15–17
    of looking vulnerable 26–7
fights, choosing your 181–3
flounders 179–80
followers, and leaders 173–6
food 53–6, 87, 181–2
friendships 124–5, 168

gender roles 121–2
Glavish, Dame Naida 141
global warming 70
godwits 173–6
gratification, instant 121
gratitude, practice of 21, 87
grief, unspoken 50–1
growth, personal 27, 97–9,
    107, 223
gut instincts 30, 31

habits 34, 223–4
*haka* (ceremonial dance) 86
Hawaiki 212
healing 25
heart
    disruption of the 17
    secrets of the 49–52
    touching the 123–5
Hinemoa 57–8
Hinemoana (ocean deity) 136
honesty 26–7
hope 157, 164
*hopo* (emotion) 16
Hui-te-Rangiora 110,
    219–22
human impact 4–5,
    10, 70–1

identity 79, 95–6, 102–3, 143,
    176, 213
ideology 93–6
imagination 21
indigenous knowledge 110–11
influencers 146
intention 33–4
intergenerational trauma 143
internalisation 45–6
intuition 30, 31

*kahikatea* (white pine) 19–21
*Kaitiakitanga* 67–115
*karakia* (prayer) 31, 86, 87,
    152–3
*karanga* (call to the spiritual
    realm) 142, 143
Kauwhata, Kato 202
kindness 32, 99
knowledge
    application of personal 113–15
    indigenous 110–11
krill 220–2
*kūmara* (sweet potato) 201–3
Kupe 211–12

labelling others 129–30
land, connection to the 5–6,
    75–7, 79
language, Māori 6, 16–17, 30,
    36–8, 54, 69–70, 78, 86,
    98–9, 148, 159–60, 175–7
leadership 185–6
    and communication skills
        191–3
    and followers 173–6
    new sense of 197–9
    self-leadership 192
learned helplessness 206
legacies 159–61
'life is for living' 209–10
listening skills 187–9
loss 50–1, 120–1, 164, 215–16
love
    being true to the love within
        you 75–9
    giving 63–4

need for 23–7
risks of 57–8
self-love 192, 199

magic of life, hidden nature
    29–32
*Manaakitanga* (support and
    hospitality towards others)
    13–64
Maniapoto, Rewi 182
Māori community 51, 64, 146
Māori language (*te reo Māori*)
    6, 16–17, 30, 36–8, 54,
    69–70, 78, 86, 98–9, 148,
    159–60, 175–7
*marae* (traditional meeting
    places) 14, 75, 77–8, 86,
    128, 142, 187–8
Mau rākau (Māori martial arts)
    127–8
mealtimes 55–6
Meat Free Mondays 160–1
mental illness 120
#metoo movement 147
Milne, Whaea Moe 76, 141
Milroy, Te Wharehuia 69–70
'mind-weeding' 45–7
mindlessness 33–4
misfortune, overcoming
    163–5
*moko kauae* (facial markings)
    30–2
mokoroa grub 19–21
moon, phases of the 47,
    89–91
mothers 141–4

nature
    closeness to 9–10
    connection with 73–4
    signs from 110
negativity 21, 33–4
New Zealand *see* Aotearoa
non-judgement 42–3
Nukutawhiti 29, 211–13
nurture 14, 23–7, 133,
    159, 192

ocean deities 87, 136, 151,
    155, 181
oceans 10, 31, 60, 68, 72, 76,
    101, 136–9, 151–3, 156,
    206, 209–10, 220, 222
    abundance of the 181–2
    pollution of the 110
octopuses 181–3
online lives 8
Ōrākau, battle of 183
outstanding individuals 35–9
overwhelm, state of 16, 26, 51,
    197, 206
oxytocin 34

Pacific Ocean (*Te Moana-
    nui-a-Kiwa*) 10, 60, 71, 155
pain 25, 42, 51, 120–1, 147,
    178, 191–2
Papatūānuku (mother earth)
    68, 76, 96
    abuse of 86
    connection to 70, 96
Pārengarenga 174
parents, new 51
*pepeha* (tribal mottos) 75–9,
    95–6, 98, 148–9
perseverance 181–3
personal growth 27, 97–9,
    107, 223
pheromones 34
plastics, single-use 10,
    71, 206
potential, reaching your 23–7
power
    hidden 29–32
    of small thing 19–21
powerlessness 182
praise, giving 59–61
prayer 31, 86, 87, 152–3
pregnancy, loss of 50–1

racism 46
Rangiātea 105–7
reciprocity 124
Reipae 95
Reitū 95

relationships 121, 124, 124–5
  end of 180
  feeling pressure to stay in 91
  negative 33–4
  spotting the dangers in 136,
    138–9
  unbreakable nature 167–9
resilience 163–5, 181–3
  manifesting 101–3
  pathways to 85
responsibilities, mutual 54–5
rock 151–3
Rongo (deity) 202
rugby 86

secrets, of the heart 49–52
self, true 32, 171–222
self-acceptance 199
self-care/nurture 14, 24–7, 192
self-doubt 16
self-judgment 130
self-kindness 32
self-leadership 192
self-love 192, 199
Shakespeare, William 160
shallowness 195
sharks 181–3
signs 135–9
silence 187–9
small things
  finding joy in 73–4
  leading to growth 97–9
  power of 19–21
social media 146–8
social support 151–3
Southern Ocean 110
spirituality 6, 45–6, 85–6,
    142–3, 152, 188
suicide 120–1

'taking a stance' 181–3
Tāne, sacred forests of 23–4,
    97–9, 164
Tangaroa (ocean deity) 136,
    151, 155, 181
Te Aru-tanga-nuku 110

teachers 35–8
*Tino rangatiratanga* 171–222
trauma, intergenerational 143
trees 216–17
truth 50
Tūmatahina 174
Turikātuku 141
Tūtanekai 57–8

Ueoneone 95
'up anchor' moments 59–61

vulnerability 26–7, 168

*waiata* (songs and chants)
    86, 148
Waiheke Island 151
Waikato 95
Waimirirangi 141
*wairua* (connection to the
    universe/spirituality/soul)
    6, 45–6, 85–6, 152, 188
*waka* (ocean-going canoes)
    37, 59–61, 82, 105,
    137, 141–4, 155,
    168, 217
*wānanga* gatherings 54
water supplies 72
wellbeing 70, 71
*whaikōrero* (speech-making)
    49–50, 128
*whakapapa* (genealogy) 60, 95,
    141
*whakataukī* 4, 6–7, 10–11
*whānau* (extended family) 4–5,
    25, 34, 46, 50–1, 55, 57–8,
    61, 77, 120, 122, 133,
    142–3, 164, 168–9, 187,
    195, 198, 206, 221
*Whanaungatanga* 117–69
wind 105–7
women 90–1, 141–4,
    159–61
words, hurtful nature 127–30

youth 90

# He Puna whakataukī/whakatauākī

*Ahakoa whati te manga, e takoto ana anō te kōhiwi* 163–5
*Aroha mai, aroha atu* 63–4

*E ea ai te werawera o Tāne tahuaroa, me heke te werawera o Tāne te wānanga* 53–6
*E kitea ai ngā taonga o te moana, me mākū koe* 209–10
*E koekoe te tūī, e ketekete te kākā, e kūkū te kererū* 41–3
*E kore au e ngaro, he kākano ahau i ruia mai i Rangiātea* 105–7
*E kore tātau e mōhio ki te waitohu nui o te wai kia mimiti rawa te puna* 69–72
*E kore te kūmara e kī ake he māngaro ia* 201–3
*E kore te pātiki e hoki ki tōna puehu* 179–80
*E ngaki ana a mua, e tōtō mai ana a muri* 45–7
*E toa ai a Whiro, me noho puku noa a Kou tangata* 205–7
*E tū te huru mā, haramai e noho. E tū te huru pango, hanatu e haere* 211–14
*Ehara i te aurukōwhao, he takerehāia!* 81–3
*Ehara! Ko koe te ringa e huti punga!* 59–61
*Ehara taku toa i te toa takitahi, engari he toa takitini* 145–9

*He aha te kai a te rangatira? He kōrero, he kōrero, he kōrero* 191–3
*He au kei uta e taea te karo, he au kei te moana e kore e taea* 135–9
*He hono tangata e kore e motu; kā pā he taura waka, e motu* 167–9
*He ihu kurī, he tangata haere* 33–4
*He iti hoki te mokoroa nāna i kakati te kahikatea* 19–21
*He kokonga whare e kitea; he kokonga ngākau e kore e kitea* 49–52
*He kuaka mārangaranga, kotahi manu e tau ki te tāhuna, tau atu, tau atu, tau atu* 173–6
*He manako te kōura i kore ai* 155–7
*He tao rākau e taea te karo, he tao kī e kore e taea* 127–30
*He toka tū moana, he ākinga nā ngā tai* 151–3

*Hōhonu kakī, pāpaku uaua* 195–6

*Ka pū te ruha, ka hao te rangatahi* 197–9
*Ka tū tonu koe i roto i te aroha* 75–9
*Ki te kotahi te kākaho, ka whati; ki te kāpuia, e kore e whati* 119–22
*Kia mate ururoa, kei mate wheke* 181–3
*Ko Atutahi te whetū tārake o te rangi* 35–9
*Ko Hinemoa, ko ahau* 57–8
*Ko ō tātou whakapono ngā kaiwehewehe i a tātau. Ko ō tātau moemoeā me ō tātau pākatokato ngā kaiwhakakotahi i a tātau* 93–6
*Ko te hoa tino pono rawa, ko tērā e toro atu ai tōna ringa ki tōu, engari ka titi kaha ki tōu manawa te kōhengihengi* 123–5
*Ko te maumahara kore ki ngā whakapapa o ōu mātua tīpuna, e rite ana ki te pūkaki awa kāore ōna hikuawa, ki te rākau rānei kāore ōna pakiaka* 131–4
*Ko te mauri, he mea huna ki te moana* 29–32
*Ko te whaea te takere o te waka* 141–4
*Kotahi karihi nāna ko te wao tapu nui a Tāne* 97–9

*Me he Ōturu ngā karu* 89–91
*Me te toroa e tau ana i runga i te au* 101–3
*Me te wai kōrari* 73–4
*Moea te wahine o te pā harakeke* 159–61

*Nā te iho ko te kōrero, nā te whakaaro nui ko te mūmū* 187–9
*Ngaro atu he tētēkura, whakaete mai he tētēkura* 185–6
*Ngaua te pae hamuti* 177–8

*Poipoia te kākano kia puāwai* 23–7

*Ruia taitea, kia tū ko taikākā* 215–17

*Tama tū, tama ora; tama noho, tama mate* 85–7
*Te manu kai miro, nōna te ngahere; te manu kai mātauranga, nōna te ao* 113–15
*Te rerenga o Hui-te-Rangiora* 219–22
*Tini whetū ki te rangi, he iti te pōkēao ka ngaro* 109–11
*Tūwhitia te hopo!* 15–17

# He mihi

## Acknowledgements

*Ehara taku toa i te toa takitahi engari, he toa takitini.*

This book has come to life through the support of many.

The inspiration of Te Wharehuia Milroy introduced me to the *aroha* for *whakataukī* and *whakatauākī*. He lives on in his many students, and I am just one of the myriad who try our best to honour his memory.

I want to acknowledge all our *kaiako reo Māori*, past, present and future, those who continue to give their all, each and every day, to ensure the sustenance and flourishing of our language. You are our *mumu reo*, our language warriors. You give us students the impetus to pass on what you have taught us. *Mei kore ake koutou hei whakamahiti korou i a mātou tō tātou reo kamehameha.*

Mum, Ina, I miss you every day. Your *aroha* is always there, guiding me on this journey.

Dad, my father John, a staunch descendent of Caroline Bay, a Professor Emeritus of physics – no slug in the writing department – you remain one of my strongest supporters, thanks Dad.

My glorious UK editor Laura, you have made this such a joyful process, *ngā mihi matihere*. And Margaret, my NZ editor, what a treat to work with you again after the *Womankind* book! Jeremy Sherlock, you were there at the beginning and helped steer the *waka* too, thank you for your generous spirit.

*E te tapairu nō Ngāti Raukawa, nō Ngati Porou anō hoki, e Hēni Jacob, ko koe te kanohi kōmiromiro. Nei a Mihi ka rere ki a koe.*

*E Rukuwai Tipene-Allen, ka kata ngā puriri o Taiamai! Ehara ehara. Te mutunga kē mai o te taunaki mai.*

*Kei a kōrua, ko Harmony Repia (Tūranga-nui-ā-Kiwa) rāua ko Luther Ashford (Ngāti Ruanui, Ngā Rauru) kāore e ārikarika ngā mihi ki a kōrua tahi ki tā kōrua mahi tōi waiwaiā.*

*E ngā kuku o taku manawa*, kids, you got mentioned at the beginning of this book and I want to acknowledge you again here. You are my heart. You are my *aroha* teachers. You know me, I'm having a *tangi* writing this. *He nui taioreore taku aroha mō kōrua tahi.*

# About the Author

Dr Hinemoa Elder has lived on Waiheke Island for more that 20 years. She is a child and adolescent psychiatrist who has worked in Starship Hospital's Child and Family and Mother, Baby Units and various community clinics. She also provides youth forensic court reports and neuropsychiatric assessment and treatment of traumatic brain injury in private practice. Hinemoa is a deputy psychiatry member of the New Zealand Mental Health Review Tribunal.

In 2019, Hinemoa was appointed a Member of the New Zealand Order of Merit, for services to psychiatry and Māori. You can also find her on Instagram @drhinemoa.

1 3 5 7 9 10 8 6 4 2

Published in 2020 by Ebury Press, an imprint of Ebury Publishing,

20 Vauxhall Bridge Road,
London SW1V 2SA

Ebury Press is part of the Penguin Random House group of companies
whose addresses can be found at global.penguinrandomhouse.com

Penguin
Random House
UK

First published by Ebury Press in 2020

www.penguin.co.uk

A CIP catalogue record for this book is available from the British Library

ISBN 9781529107067

Cover design by Sophie Yamamoto
Page design by Seagull.Net
Typeset by Jouve (UK), Milton Keynes
Colour origination by BORN Ltd
Printed and bound in Great Britain by Clays Ltd, Elcograf S.p.A.

MIX
Paper from
responsible sources
FSC® C018179

Penguin Random House is committed to a
sustainable future for our business, our readers
and our planet. This book is made from Forest
Stewardship Council® certified paper.